Women's
The View from t₁

by Carolyn G. Heilbrun

Eve has been supposed to have remarked to Adam as they left the garden, my dear, we are in a state of transition, and of course they were. It is no coincidence that Eve delivers this line. While humanity in every era and stage in history has been marked by a strong sense of itself as being in a state of transition, women have always had a particularly close relationship to changeable terrain. In their quest for self knowledge, boundaries, and names, women have found themselves between varying cultural demands. In one view, perhaps the dominant one, the only way to gain positive status is to fit appropriately into approved categories: appropriately beautiful, appropriately young, appropriately thin, appropriately successful. In another view, the view compellingly expressed by Carolyn Heilbrun, women must abandon the appropriate and seek out the liminal. The word limen means threshold. To be in a state of liminality is to be poised upon uncertain ground, on the brink of leaving one condition or country or self to enter upon another. When recognized, liminality offers women freedom to be or become themselves.

In *Women's Lives: The View from the Threshold*, Carolyn Heilbrun looks at the biographies and memoirs of women who have wrestled with their own betwixt and betweenness (in the process altering the face of literature, and world): George Eliot, Virginia Woolf, Willa Cather, Harriet Beecher Stowe, and Gloria Steinem. She reveals the ways in which feminism has changed our perceptions of these lives. Surprising explorations of the positions which launch women into uncertain ground extend these lectures outside the academic purview.

Each year the Alexander lectureship invites a distinguished scholar to the University of Toronto to give a course of public lectures on the subject of English Literature. These four lectures from the 1997 series put Carolyn Heilbrun in a line of distinguished scholarly work with such previous lecturers as Walter Ong, Robertson Davies, and Northrop Frye. But Heilbrun, within this distinguished genealogy, reworks the very notion of the line, creating a new pattern of writing and approaching literary culture, just as the women whose lives she examines have done. The reader will come out of this experience moved, refreshed, and inspired to create rather than take a position.

THE ALEXANDER LECTURES

The Alexander Lectureship was founded in honour of Professor W.J. Alexander, who held the Chair of English at University College, University of Toronto, from 1889 to 1926. Each year the Lectureship brings to the University a distinguished scholar or critic to give a course of lectures on a subject related to English Literature.

Women's Lives

The View from
the Threshold

CAROLYN G. HEILBRUN

UNIVERSITY OF TORONTO PRESS
Toronto Buffalo London

© Carolyn G. Heilbrun 1999
Published by the University of Toronto Press Incorporated
Toronto Buffalo London
Printed in Canada

ISBN 0-8020-4428-X (cloth)
ISBN 0-8020-8228-9 (paper)

∞

Printed on acid-free paper

Canadian Cataloguing in Publication Data

Heilbrun, Carolyn G., 1926–
Women's lives : the view from the threshold

(The Alexander lectures)
ISBN 0-8020-4428-X (bound)   ISBN 0-8020-8228-9 (pbk.)

1. Women authors, English – Biography – History and criticism.
2. Women authors, American – Biography – History and criticism.
3. Eliot, George, 1819–1880 – Criticism, interpretation, etc.
4. Woolf, Virginia, 1882–1941 – Criticism, interpretation, etc.
5. Cather, Willa, 1873–1947 – Criticism, interpretation, etc.
6. Stowe, Harriet Beecher, 1811–1896 – Criticism, interpretation, etc.
7. Feminism and literature.   8. Feminist literary criticism.
I. Title.   II. Series.

PR111.H453 1999   820.9′287   C98-932971-2

University of Toronto Press acknowledges the financial assistance to
its publishing program of the Canada Council for the Arts and the
Ontario Arts Council.

*To those who invited me to give the Alexander Lectures
and who made my stay in Toronto so pleasurable*

CONTENTS

CHAPTER ONE

Deliciously Hideous, A Powerful Beauty

It is possible that every era and stage in human history has considered itself to be in a state of transition. Eve has been supposed to have remarked to Adam as they left the garden, 'My dear, we are in a state of transition,' and indeed they were. The sort of transition I shall be speaking about in these four lectures is more exactly defined as a threshold experience, that is, as providing to the actors involved the condition of liminality. The word 'limen' means 'threshold,' and to be in a state of liminality is to be poised upon uncertain ground, to be leaving one condition or country or self and entering upon another. But the most salient sign of liminality is its unsteadiness, its lack of clarity about exactly where one belongs and what one should be doing, or wants to be doing.

From the first moment when I began to think about what I would say in these lectures, it seemed to me obvious that I must speak of how feminism, beginning in the late sixties and still reverberating today, although in different form, has affected the literature I have studied and taught for the almost half-century of my professional and pre-professional life. The fact I soon came to recognize is that the way in which we read all literature has been indelibly transformed by the feminist interpretations. Feminism, in literature as in life, has either moved women, or tried to move them, from the margins closer to the centre of human experience and possibility or has made evident their absence from that centre.

I actually began with a rather simple and far less sweeping idea; I thought I would confine myself to biographies of women, and devote each of my four lectures to a woman biographical subject, discussing and revealing how views of her life and work had been transformed by feminism. In each case, I was interested only in comparing excellent, highly regarded literary works written before and after feminism.

The four figures I thought to study through comparative biographies and speak to you about in each of my lectures were George Eliot, Virginia Woolf, Willa Cather, and Harriet Beecher Stowe. In the case of Stowe, I was able to compare two biographies that had each won the Pulitzer Prize: the first by Forrest Wilson in 1942 (characteristically titled *Crusader in Crinoline* – I had to look the book up in the library to determine its subject), the second by Joan Hedrick in 1994. Speaking of women in the margins, it is perhaps worth noting that the Hedrick biography of Stowe received only the third Pulitzer Prize given for the biography of a woman by a woman since the prize was initiated in 1917. The very first Pulitzer in biography went to the daughters of Julia Ward Howe for a biography of her (she is the author of 'The Battle Hymn of the Republic,' among other achievements). The second, in 1986, went to Elizabeth Frank for the biography of Louise Bogan; Bogan was not a feminist, to say the least, but the prize would hardly have been given before the feminist movement. And then, in 1994, we had the new biography of Stowe, which is certainly feminist, though I suspect the Pulitzer judges of agreeing to overlook that fact since the subject was so solidly 'American.'

I assumed that if the two Pulitzer Prize biographies of Stowe were to be compared, such transformations as might be revealed would be a matter of deep interest. I found, however, that the interest was real but not profound, largely because the changes were so obvious as to need no feminist to point them out. Examples of these changes were, first, a deeper understanding throughout the later work that the demands made upon housewives, such as those made upon both Stowe herself and her mother, took terrible tolls on women's health. Second, the frank recognition that the lack of contraception meant that women's bodies were weakened by a continuous state of pregnancy: Harriet Stowe's mother, in fact, died young from both too much domestic labour and too frequent births. Hedrick also had access to new materials; it was evident, however, that Forrest Wilson, like many other male biographers of accomplished women, was far less frightened of evident ambition and ambivalence towards wifely demands than were women biographers of women in that pre-feminist period. Although the Hedrick biography was far more complete and contemporary, there was no profound disagreement between her and Forrest Wilson.

As I hope you have guessed by now, I abandoned the idea of limiting my analysis to the development within distinct genres. It became clear to me that I had to speak much more generally about feminism and literature. I had, somewhat to my astonishment, discovered that the chief characteristic of the literature and the writers I surveyed, and the chief theme of my lectures, was the liminality I described at the beginning of this evening's talk. But before I elaborate upon my major idea, let me make what seems to me a significant point, particularly since I will be speaking, after this interlude, almost entirely of women and of the literature they create.

Not all feminist literary revisions were by women. One

of the earlier and most significant feminist insights, in my opinion, appeared in an article on Conrad's *Heart of Darkness* published by Garrett Stewart in 1980.[1] You will remember that, at the end of *Heart of Darkness*, after Marlow has found Kurtz and watched him die, Marlow returns to England and calls upon Kurtz's 'intended.' He lies to her about Kurtz's life, and especially about his death, telling her that Kurtz's last words were of her. (Kurtz's last words were, of course, 'The Horror, the Horror.') Mr Stewart points out that Marlow had earlier said he hated a lie above all, that '"[w]hether political, moral, or psychological, mendacity is the most mortal of sins, against ourselves and others"' (319).

By lying to the Intended, Marlow violates his own spiritual insight into imperialism. As Stewart notes, *Heart of Darkness* is 'in part a political autopsy of imperialist myths' (ibid). And central to the 'myth' is Marlow's view of women: 'It is queer how out of touch with truth women are,' Marlow says. 'They live in a world of their own, and there has never been anything like it, and never can be. It is too beautiful altogether, and if they were to set it up it would go to pieces before the first sunset. Some confounded fact we men have been living contentedly with ever since the day of creation would start up and knock the whole thing over.'[2]

This comment stands beside Marlow's description of imperialism: 'The conquest of the earth, which mostly means the taking it away from those who have a different complexion or slightly flatter noses than ourselves, is not a pretty thing when you look into it too much' (7). It is, indeed, exactly the sort of 'confounded fact men have been living contentedly with ever since the day of creation,' or at any rate, the day when Cain killed Abel. And lying to women about this is not only essential to imperialism; keeping women ignorant and dependent upon men for truth is essential to keeping the system of imperialism and patriarchy intact. Therefore, although Conrad critics before Stewart all excused Marlow's lie to the Intended as a 'white lie,' Stewart's stunning insight allowed us to realize that at the very heart of imperialism and the conquering of new-found countries for their riches like ivory and gold lurks the patriarchy which lies to women and refuses them a part in ongoing life. Conrad himself, as Stewart also reveals, consciously or unconsciously understood that lying to women was at the very heart of imperialism, and that its practice amounted to moral death.

In the years that followed, feminism introduced into the study of modernism the recognition that fear of women, of their voices and their new-found power – however incomplete that power, however hesitant those voices – was the single most forceful motivation behind male modernist literature. I shall not expand upon that point here; it has been brilliantly illustrated by Gilbert and Gubar's three-volume *No Man's Land*,[3] where they describe how literature before and after the First World War amounted, on the part of male writers, to a virtual war of the sexes. Women were seen by men as invasive, evil, challenging male domination, and intruding upon men's right to be recognized as the only genuine creators of literature. A moment's review of the modernist writer's canon, apart, of course, from the Bloomsbury Group, will suggest what

I am speaking of here. Writers from H. Rider Haggard and
Max Beerbohm to T.S. Eliot, D.H. Lawrence, and James
Joyce demonstrate that, for them, as for Marlow, women
appear in these male modernist masterpieces as beyond
the range of human experience, existing not as subjects of
their own fates, but as objects of men's desire or detesta-
tion, and not infrequently as both at once.

Feminism both revealed this and, as women set out to
write, revised it. Women began to portray the new possi-
bilities that, as a result of feminism, they found themselves confronting. They began to question, as I shall, all
strictures about women and about the institutions in which
women now, in ever greater numbers, and in a state of
awakening, found themselves.

For the most part, they found themselves betwixt and
between, neither altogether here nor there, not one kind
of person or another, not this, not that. They found themselves in a state of liminality, and this state is very well
expressed in recent women's memoirs which I shall discuss in a later lecture. But to give you the feeling now of
what I mean by liminality, by being somehow off centre, I
want to offer you a few illustrations from a contemporary
memoir, called *Thirty-Six Views of Mount Fuji* after paint-
ings by the Japanese artist Hokusai. It is the account of
Cathy Davidson, a professor of English at Duke University who has spent much time teaching in Japan, and who
felt torn between the two cultures. In America, she missed
Japan; in Japan, she had to recognize that she would
never be really at home, never master the language or the
customs. She came to realize that it was as a visitor to
Japan that she was able to savour her liminal position. In

the end she returned to North Carolina and there built a Japanese-style home.

I knew, she writes, that 'no matter how hard I might try to understand this new culture, to fit in as gracefully as possible, at times I was going to fail. There would be many ... embarrassing or painful moments, misunderstandings, conflicts, confusion, frustration ... I was seeing Japan, but I was also seeing myself again, inside out, viewed as well as viewing. This, I thought, is what it means to be a foreigner.'[4]

'Intensity, novelty, urgency, surprise: that's what it means to be ... in foreign territory, slightly forbidden, hard to categorize,' (22) a definition of liminality I ask you to remember.

The whole idea of liminality arose in rituals and festivals; I shall go into this more completely in a later lecture, but suffice it now to say that what one does in these rituals or festivals is enact a role one would never dream of in one's usual, ordinary life. Here is Cathy Davidson in Japan waiting with friends at a bus stop in the rain, where there are other Japanese also waiting. She is suddenly moved to dance Gene Kelly's dance from *Singing in the Rain*.

'I think we're frightening these people,' [her friend whispered.]

'Do you think they would have been as frightened if I were a Japanese instead of a [foreigner] dancing in the rain?'

'I think only a [foreigner] would have tap-danced in the rain' [he said].

'But I did it *because* I'm a [foreigner]. Back in America, I would have waited quietly and respectfully with the other passengers ... At times, when I'm in Japan, I feel freer than I do in America, more irresponsible.' (23)

As a visiting professor at a prestigious Japanese college, Davidson was in a somewhat unusual position for a woman. As she notes,

In professional contexts, more than one Japanese woman remarked that I was often spoken of and to with forms of respect reserved for men in Japan ... When I pushed the issue, they also admitted that, if I was respected, it might be because in some sense I didn't really count. I was from another world, beyond the pale of professional competition, outside the battle of the sexes ... It was as if my foreignness put me in some different gender category, on one level proximate and titillating, on another androgynous and remote. (88)

This description will serve to help us re-envision the life of another woman who entered what was for her a strange place, one perhaps as strange as Japan to Davidson. Her name was to be George Eliot, and the new culture she encountered was the culture of those women whose very survival depended upon their being considered good-looking. Mary Ann Evans had, most unusually for her time, come from the country to establish herself as a solitary professional woman in London; as a plain or homely woman, she found herself on the threshold of a society controlled by those for whom women's personal beauty was paramount.

Certainly we have all been trained to call George Eliot a homely, even an ugly, woman. Here is how Henry James, writing to his father, described her:

> To begin with she is magnificently ugly – deliciously hideous. She has a low forehead, a dull grey eye, a vast pendulous nose, a huge mouth, full of uneven teeth ... Now in this vast ugliness resides a most powerful beauty which, in a very few minutes steals forth and charms the mind, so that you end as I ended, in falling in love with her. Yes, behold me literally in love with this great horse-faced blue-stocking. I don't know in what the charm lies, but it is thoroughly potent ... Altogether she has a larger circumference than any woman I have ever seen.[5]

And he is not there speaking of her physical girth, but of the magnitude of her presence.

Her biographer Gordon Haight – and his biography of her is a very great work indeed – mentioned that on one occasion she wept, knowing she was not beautiful. In her youth she refers in letters to her 'ugliness,' writing 'I am a hideous hag.' Herbert Spencer – a perfectly dreadful man, in my opinion, both for his ideas of Social Darwinism (the weak should be left to die while the strong triumph) and for his ideas on female beauty – wrote on the importance of beauty. He illustrated ugliness by describing features that Marian Evans knew herself to possess, and declaring 'a *necessary* relationship between ugly features and inferiority of intellect and character' (115). In her case, this was obviously the opposite of the truth, but such opinions have long influenced us all.

Haight, if he did not sympathize with cruel remarks

about George Eliot's lack of beauty, nonetheless saw her as a woman unable to endure alone. The dominant motif of her life, he insisted, was that 'she was not fitted to stand alone, always requiring someone to lean upon.' That 'someone' is, of course, presumed to be a man. Professor Phyllis Rose, writing in 1983, responded to Haight's analysis of Eliot in this way:

> What I see is a woman of passionate nature who struggles, amidst limited opportunity, to find someone to love and to love her; a woman who goes to quite unconventional lengths and is willing to be unusually aggressive – almost predatory – in her efforts to secure for herself what she wants. To want love and sex in one's life is hardly, after all, a sign of neurosis. And is it a sign of dependence for a woman to want love and sex from a man? It is a small matter of emphasis only, but it does seem to me to make some difference whether we think of one of the most powerful female writers ever as neurotically dependent on men or as brave enough to secure for herself what she wanted.[6]

Such a reinterpretation supposes that even women not adjudged beautiful can, if they resist being nothing more than an object to be viewed by men, manage their sexual and marital lives.

Virginia Woolf, perhaps, understood Eliot, if not better, from another angle:

> She never wrote a story until she was thirty-seven, and by the time she was thirty-seven she had come to think of

herself with a mixture of pain and something like resentment. For long she preferred not to think of herself at all. Then, when the first flush of creative energy was exhausted and self-confidence had come to her, she wrote more and more from the personal standpoint, but she did so without the unhesitating abandonment of the young. Her self-consciousness is always marked when her heroines say what she herself would have said. She disguised them in every possible way. She granted them beauty and wealth into the bargain ... But the disconcerting and stimulating fact remained that she was compelled by the very power of her genius to step forth in person upon the quiet bucolic scene.[7]

And that person was male.

Virginia Woolf understood all this because, although clearly beautiful herself, as photographs and contemporaries amply testify, she disliked looking at herself, and all her life avoided mirrors, detested shopping and trying on clothes, and dressed with evident carelessness. Confidence in one's beauty is a 'sometime thing' and, even in women professionally beautiful, must be replenished, redone, constantly attended to.

When I began teaching English literature thirty-five years ago, few women authors were considered worth studying, and I had very few women colleagues, at least in graduate school. Certainly, Virginia Woolf herself was not considered worthy of serious masculine attention, that is, the attention of male professors and the women who wished to join them. Here is how Virginia Woolf responded to the fulminations of one such woman critic:

'Oh, I've had such a drubbing and a scourging from the Cambridge ladies,' she wrote to Ethel Smyth in 1938, after publishing *Three Guineas*. 'I'm a disgrace to my sex; and a caterpillar on the community. I thought I should raise their hackles – poor old strumpets.' Queenie Leavis had written: 'Mrs. Woolf's latest effort is a let-down for our sex ... this book is not merely silly and ill-informed, though it is that too, it contains some dangerous assumptions, some preposterous claims and some nasty attitudes ... It seems to me the art of living as conceived by a social parasite.'[8]

Men, and the women like Mrs Leavis who spoke for them, flourished for decades in both England and America. In the United States, Woolf did not become a recognized subject for serious critical study until well into the 1970s, while in England, as Hermione Lee reports in her new biography, Woolf was not studied in her English course at Oxford. Lee writes that, '[a]t graduate level, she was described to me by my tutor as a minor modernist, not to be classed with Joyce, Eliot or Lawrence,' and, Lee admits, that was how she thought of Woolf for some years. I myself was told in graduate school that Woolf had simply copied *Mrs. Dalloway* from *Ulysses*, so there was no point in seriously considering it. Close to sixty years later, Woolf and feminism – the word she could never bring herself to use publicly – have at last taken their proper place within literary criticism and biography.

John Berger's now famous statement, 'men look at women and women watch themselves being looked at,' is about the most concise history of women that can be found anywhere, and it refers back to the beginning of recorded history. At the same time, women who dared to put their energies into writing, rather than directing all their attention towards pleasing men, were considered 'not worth looking at,' either as authors or as women. Women themselves, meanwhile, looking everywhere – in literature, culture, religion, history – for role models, discovered – or, as it rather seems, always knew – that all the role models were male. Women's history, if they had any, consisted in their being beautiful enough to become events in male lives. The only role models women could find were in the magazines, and, in our day, in movies and television. These models were, of course, all beautiful, thin, young, and exquisitely made up. What else was there?

In 1991 Naomi Wolf published a book called *The Beauty Myth*, which is the best account of how women's need for beauty and for being looked at by men with admiration costs women in industrialized countries everything from money to time to self-denigration and despair. No magazine for women will feature any subject that advertisers of beauty products for women do not approve, and that are not aimed at the young, often the very young. In a recent book about women's lives, the author begins with this 'event of significance: A man of my own age, with whom I was talking at a party, withdrew his attention from me to look hungrily over my shoulder at a pretty young woman many years my junior ... I saw very clearly, in that instant when the man's gaze shifted, that one kind of power had passed from me. The time had come to develop other resources.'[9] It is true that the French are supposed to have a type of woman called a *jolie laide*, but that is just to say that if you try hard enough you may do even better for yourself than God could have done if he had taken the trouble.

Now why am I telling you all this? Why do I consider questions about the beauty of women, or the lack thereof, suitable to these reputable and highly dignified lectures? For two reasons, at least to start with. The first is rather simple. I don't believe that such homely women as occur in our history and literature, or such women as are judged less beautiful than the woman offered in contrast, have ever been marshalled before us to receive our acclaim and accolades. My second reason is to suggest what has never before, to my knowledge, been explored: that lacking beauty may for some women be a secret clue to power, accomplishment, self-esteem, and even success with men, if of a somewhat unconventional kind.

How do we define not-beautiful, homely, whatever we are to call it? Several definitions leap to mind: 'not beautiful' as a neutral designation; decidedly unattractive, even ugly; unfeminine, or masculine. What of the beautiful woman who believes herself not beautiful, or who dislikes the reification of her beauty and downplays it? Is it ever possible for a woman to be so unaffected by her looks that she really doesn't think about it? This last, I suggest, occurs only in middle age, on the part of those women who happily desert the desire to be looked at; it is an unlikely condition in the young. How much of a sense of self can a woman attain who is successfully regarded as beautiful in the heterosexual world? Yeats, we remember, held out little hope:

Never shall a young man,
Thrown into despair
By those great honey-colored
Ramparts at your ear,
Love you for yourself alone
And not your yellow hair ...

I heard an old religious man
But yesternight declare
That he had found a text to prove
That only God, my dear,
Could love you for yourself alone
And not your yellow hair.[10]

We must also remember that, apart from Gloria Steinem
and Germaine Greer, any woman in the early days of this
feminist movement who declared herself a feminist was
immediately regarded as ugly, or unsuccessful in attracting men, or a lesbian. Steinem was such a threat to many
men and women because she could have had what all
women are supposed to want and declined it all.

Our memories of women so often privilege their failure
to be beautiful or to be mothers, ignoring the while what
may have been their extensive success as accomplished
people in one field or another. Queen Elizabeth I is an
obvious example. She was a remarkable ruler. As Trevelyan
has put it in his history of England, 'With a hope too like
despair men turned passionately to a young woman to
save them, the third and last of Henry's progeny, of whom
two had failed their need; by the strangest chance in

history, no elder statesman or famous captain in all broad
Europe would have served so well to lead Englishmen
back to harmony and prosperity and on to fresh fields of
fame.'[11]

But whole plays have been written comparing Elizabeth unfavourably with Mary Queen of Scots, a despi-
cable human being and a murderer, because Mary was
beautiful and the mother of a son. Elizabeth was once
heard to envy Mary that son and heir to the English
throne, and that single recorded regret has ramified beyond all Elizabeth's great achievements as Queen, just as
her love of Essex and handsome young men is seen only
as an admission of her supposedly sad female destiny.

With George Eliot, it is much the same. John Chapman
believed her looks would lead only to despair. Reporting
on a conversation with Marian Evans, not yet George
Eliot, he wrote in his diary, that on a country walk, he
'dwelt also on the incomprehensible mystery and witch-
ery of beauty. My words jarred upon her and put an end
to her enjoyment. Was it from a consciousness of her own
want of beauty? She wept bitterly.'[12] John Chapman, we
may remember, was a literary personage who made Eliot
editor of his journal, the *Westminster Review*, and in whose
house she lived when she first moved, alone, to London
to search for a possible life. She soon found that life.
'Marian was at last in her element,' Rosemary Ashton
writes today.'It suited her to be meeting the leading lib-
eral thinkers of the day, most of whom shared her views
on religion and politics, but none of whom was – as she
saw clearly enough – superior to her in intelligence and
knowledge. She reveled in her backroom role of adviser

and organizer, knowing that she could boss Chapman to good effect, and finding too, that she had a store of tact which she could use successfully on Chapman and others.'[13]

About this same time, the 'young woman who had so often been in despair about her future – emotional, social, and intellectual – thus sat thoroughly enjoying a bad performance of one of Shakespeare's lesser plays in the company of the three men who had been, or were shortly to be, in the closest possible relation to her in all three respects' ([Ashton,] 94). The three men were Herbert Spencer, John Chapman, and George Henry Lewes. Before she met Lewes, with whom she lived for the rest of his life, she had been in love with Herbert Spencer, who assured himself he could not marry, despite his extensive admiration for her, because of her lack of beauty. But he also did not marry Beatrice Potter, who was good-looking, nor, indeed, anyone else: he died a bachelor. George Eliot, in an amazing love letter, begged him not to marry anyone else if he could not marry her, but few have taken time to notice that he never did. One can only speculate, but it is possible, perhaps likely, that she had had sexual relations with both Spencer and Chapman.

Neither George Eliot herself nor anyone who knew her had any doubts about the fact that she was not beautiful, that her face must be judged on a spectrum between ugly and gross. We have seen how Henry James described her. George Eliot referred to herself as a medusa, the mythical woman so ugly that any man who looked upon her was turned to stone, or so the story went (Jane Harrison had quite another interpretation, describing Medusa as originally 'a potent goddess, not as in later days a monster to be slain by heroes').[14] Maggie Tulliver as a child with wild hair is called a medusa. The real definition of a medusa is a woman men cannot control, and therefore fear. (For Freud, not unexpectedly, the medusa stood for the female genitals, threatening men and suggesting what could happen to them if they didn't watch out.)

But, like James, those who got to know George Eliot came to esteem her face. Bessie Parkes, one of Eliot's close women friends, wrote in a letter: 'As I know her better, the harsh heavy look of her face softens into a very beautiful tender expression.' Blackwood, Eliot's publisher who, because of her wish for anonymity, did not meet her for a long time, wrote to his partner once he and Eliot did meet: 'She is a most intelligent, pleasant woman, with a face like a man, but a good expression.'[15]

I want to look somewhat more closely at George Eliot's life to understand both the price her plainness cost her and the rewards her lack of beauty won her. It is certainly true that, for much of her life, Eliot was anxious, depressed, even fearful. But though her looks may have accounted for some of this during her youthful unhappiness, once she went to live with Lewes, her misery clearly arose from other causes: her anomalous social position in living with a man to whom she was not married, a very serious social crime and the cause of her ostracism at that time; all the problems connected with her anonymity; the brutal rejection she suffered from her family, and particularly her brother Isaac. Before she became George Eliot, however, when she was still Marian Evans, and before that Mary Ann Evans, her lack of beauty can, I believe, be seen as the most salient factor in making possible her extraordinary life.

Ashton tells us that George Eliot's 'was a difficult lot, to be so intelligent as to attract the amazed attention of men, but to find that her attraction for most of them was purely intellectual, not physical' (49). This is a statement with which we more or less automatically concur. All women, and not even a young George Eliot was an exception, feel rejected and unworthy if men do not evidently desire them. Yet the reverse condition is too little contemplated. In her recently published autobiography, Katharine Graham, the owner of the *Washington Post,* notes that her mother was a stunningly beautiful woman whose husband decided to marry her once he had caught sight of her; he did not even defer this decision until they had met or held a conversation with each other. This woman, Graham's mother, in later years remarked on her youth, in which she was so successful in attracting men: 'This gift, to be beloved by various males,' she said, 'made me conceited and self-centered to an unbelievable degree ... For several years to come I was in love chiefly with myself, an ecstasy that cost me and others much pain before life cured me of this intoxication.' Her daughter adds, 'Not to put too fine a point on it, life had hardly cured her of her self-absorption.'[16] Clearly, beauty seldom develops a character like George Eliot's.

Without doubt, George Eliot's plainness allowed her to undertake adventures too daring for the usual young woman. As Ashton puts it, 'it was certainly not usual for respectable unmarried women to take lodgings or holidays alone ... It is likely that Marian relied, as she had hoped to do in Geneva [where she had also taken lodgings alone], on her serious demeanour and her looking older than she was to save her from social embarrassment' (100). Her serious demeanour and belief that she looked older than she was were both the products of her plainness; that plainness protected her not only from conventions, but from the unsought attentions of casual men. For reasons inherent in all patriarchal societies, to be noticed by accidentally encountered men – anyone from construction workers to those met at elegant parties – is always assumed to be welcomed by women, and often is. Yet the protection rewarded for plainness is not to be demeaned. Tess of the d'Urbervilles, we may remember, cut off her eyebrows in an attempt to look less beautiful and less tempting to men. Nor would Tess have been seduced and given birth to a baby named Sorrow were it not for her allure.

Yet the young George Eliot, unlike Charlotte Lucas in *Pride and Prejudice*, did not marry a man she did not love or who was insufficiently intelligent, just because he had proposed to her. She knew what she wanted from love, and life gave it to her. As Ashton observes, 'Once more a stubborn independence of spirit did battle with her fear of loneliness and insecurity, and won' (70). Her friends, who, needless to say, had worried that she was not married, were later anxious about her relationship with Lewes, not only because it was not a legal marriage, but also because Lewes had a reputation for wildness. 'All Marian's friends, male and female, feared – that Lewes would "tire of & put away Miss Evans – as he has done others"' (125). (George Henry Lewes, in fact, was a model of genuine morality.

He continued all his life, and George Eliot continued after his death, to support the children his legal wife had with Thornton Hunt.)

Of course, she was lonely when she was young. She wrote to her friend Cara Bray, 'I can't help losing belief that people love me – the unbelief is in my nature and no sort of fork will drive it finally out' (Ashton, 180). This, and not the lack of attention from passing males, is the price for plainness, and when it was joined to her irregular marital situation and to her anonymity as a writer, it continued forcefully to affect her. By the time she wrote *Adam Bede*, she was able to allow the narrator the observation that, if Amos Barton was no better looking than the average, 'Bless us, things may be lovable that are not altogether handsome, I hope.' And when she was at the end of her life, she responded to a letter from a young man who had described his yearning for love: 'especially I know the blighting effect on the sympathies of an unsatisfied yearning for a supreme engrossing affection' (305). Yet she recognized, once that supreme engrossing affection had been bestowed upon her, '[f]ew women I fear have had such reason as I have to think the long sad years of youth were worth living for the sake of middle age' (187). If it was her plainness that was largely responsible for the 'long sad years of youth,' they paid off handsomely, as I have noticed they often do, in middle age. We may also surmise that her lack of feminine wiles and girlish prettiness made the arguments with her father and brother likelier, and thus freed her, however unhappily, to explore the world and find a life better suited to her great talents.

George Eliot, when it comes to her fictional women however, transforms what life has taught her. With the possible exception of Mary Garth (and would so feckless a chap as Fred Vincy really have loved her forever?), all of George Eliot's heroines are deeply attractive. True, *Daniel Deronda* begins with Daniel wondering about the attractions of the woman we will soon know as Gwendolen Harleth: 'Was she beautiful or not beautiful? and what was the secret of form or expression which gave the dynamic quality to her glance?' Like Scarlet O'Hara, whose comeliness is also mentioned in the novel's first sentence ('Scarlet O'Hara was not beautiful but men seldom realized it when caught by her charm'), there is no real question in either case, nor do we need to wait beyond the first sentence of *Middlemarch* – 'Miss Brooke had that kind of beauty which seems to be thrown into relief by poor dress' – to have Dorothea's pulchritude established. The lack of beauty is too difficult a problem for George Eliot, it seems. She could not draw on her own experience in portraying any of her women protagonists, with the exception of Maggie Tulliver as a child, and she, too, grows into gorgeous womanhood before dying.

Elizabeth Gaskell, in her biography of Charlotte Brontë, demonstrates that Charlotte Brontë was determined not to impose beauty on her protagonists: 'She once told her sisters that they were wrong – even morally wrong – in making their heroines beautiful as a matter of course. They replied that it was impossible to make a heroine interesting on any other terms. Her answer was, "I will prove to you that you are wrong; I will show you a heroine as plain and as small as myself, who shall be as interesting as any of yours."'[17]

George Smith, Charlotte Brontë's publisher, is reported to have said of her that she would willingly have traded all her genius to be beautiful. This is a characteristic displacement. I do not believe this; would most women – and I ask this further question sincerely – prefer to be beautiful when young or to have written two novels at least that have changed the lives and entranced millions of people? That to have written *Jane Eyre* and *Villette* should even for a moment be considered too large a price to pay for not being beautiful seems to me preposterous. But it would not seem so to many and, alas, probably not to young women as yet unsure of their talent and hungry for immediate, if transient, satisfactions. Charlotte Brontë was, like her sisters, solitary, but she described her unhappiness clearly in a letter to Ellen Nussey: 'The evils that now and then wring a groan from my heart, lie in my position, not that I am a *single* woman and like to remain a *single* woman, but because I am a *lonely* woman and likely to be lonely.'[18] We might add that Charlotte Brontë was completing *Villette* as she wrote that letter.

I shall offer you only one more example at the moment, this one from a male author. In Wilkie Collins's *The Woman in White*, the woman who will be the female hero – one can hardly say the heroine, that role being reserved for a very pretty, very helpless, sweet, and uninformed young lady – is introduced thus by the male hero:

> I looked from the table to the window farthest from me, and saw a lady standing at it, with her back turned towards me. The instant my eyes rested on her, I was struck by the rare beauty of her form, and by the unaffected grace of her attitude. Her figure was tall yet not too tall; comely

and well-developed, yet not fat; her head set on her shoulders with an easy, pliant firmness; her waist, perfection in the eyes of a man ... was visibly and delightfully undeformed by stays ... She turned toward me immediately ... She left the window – and I said to myself, The lady is dark. She moved forward a few steps – and I said to myself, The lady is young. She approached nearer – and I said to myself ..., The lady is ugly!

He goes on to describe her as swarthy, with a large, firm, masculine mouth and jaw, 'and the dark down on her upper lip was almost a moustache.'[19] This woman, Marion Halcombe, is a new creation in literature, a creation for which, when Collins wrote, there was no precedent, no place, certainly no name. She was not the heroine; she was not the hero, that place being reserved for Walter Hartright, who will love the sweet, feminine sister of Miss Halcombe; she is altogether original. She will not be unloved, for the wonderful villain Count Fosco will admire her profoundly, but she will end up holding the baby of the two principals, with no future role in sight save that of maiden aunt. Like the ending, the first sentence of the book denies her existence in the narrative: 'This is the story of what a Woman's patience can endure, and what a man's resolution can achieve.' No Marian Halcombe there. Still, she has been created, she has been thought up.

Female beauty in itself is not harmful; on the contrary, it must inevitably be greeted with pleasure and delight in nature's ability to surprise us with flawlessness. As E.M. Forster put it in a quite other connection, sometimes 'nature remembers the physical perfection that she accomplished elsewhere, and throws out a god – not many, but one here and there, to prove to society how little its categories impress her.'[20] What becomes harmful is when beauty becomes not only an ideal but a standard expected of every woman – a standard, moreover, which no woman can quite attain, not even the actress, for example, who embodies it. She, too, must resort to cosmetic surgery, purging diets, and other tortures in order to fit the ideal her youth allowed her to portray or, if she is still young, an ideal beyond what she has attained. A Marilyn Monroe and a Greta Garbo have each been remoulded nearer to the heart's desire; Hollywood's heart, that is.

As long as woman was designed to be an appendage to man, with no higher aim in life than to be looked at with pleasure, she hardly seems fit to serve as the protagonist of great literature. Liminality, I assert, is necessary for that destiny. That is why the women novelists I have discussed grant a profound complexity to their heroines – if they are beautiful – to compensate for that necessary but questionable gift.

At the end of Virginia Woolf's *Mrs. Dalloway*, that novel's heroine, over fifty, transforms herself from Mrs Richard Dalloway to Clarissa Dalloway. And at the very end of the book, which can be seen as a journey through liminality, Peter Walsh watches as she stands before him, the reborn individual. 'What is this terror? What is this ecstasy? he thought to himself. What is it that fills me with extraordinary excitement? It is Clarissa, he said. For there she was.'

Thus, for women, the first experience of liminality may come, not when they regret that they are insufficiently thin, elegant, beautiful, but when, recognizing that be-

cause of eccentric natural endowments, or ageing, or any
failure to conform to the current ideal of female beauty,
they have reached that essential female stage of liminality.
Such women recognize their betwixt-and-betweenness,
gaze steadily upon their failure to have achieved or chosen to remain in a conventional destiny, and, welcoming
their liminality, use it, as George Eliot and Charlotte Brontë
did, to explore another way of female life. They invent, in
that liminality, freedom as a woman to be or to become
herself.

NOTES

1 Garrett Stewart, 'Lying as Dying in *Heart of Darkness*,' *PMLA* 95/3
   (May 1980): 319–30.
2 Joseph Conrad, *Heart of Darkness* (New York: Norton Critical
   Edition, 1971), 12.
3 Sandra M. Gilbert and Susan Gubar, *No Man's Land*, vol. 1: *The
   War of the Words* (New Haven, CT, and London: Yale University
   Press, 1987).
4 Cathy N. Davidson, *Thirty-Six Views of Mount Fuji* (New York:
   Dutton, 1993), 12–13.
5 Gordon S. Haight, *George Eliot: A Biography* (London and New
   York: Oxford University Press, 1968), 417.
6 Phyllis Rose, *Parallel Lives: Five Victorian Marriages* (New York:
   Knopf, 1983), 211.
7 Virginia Woolf, 'George Eliot,' *The Common Reader* (New York:
   Harcourt Brace, 1925; rpt. 1948), 238.
8 *The Letters of Virginia Woolf*, ed. Nigel Nicolson and Joanne
   Trautmann (New York: Harcourt Brace Jovanovich, 1980), 271.
9 Kennedy Fraser, *Ornament and Silence: Essays on Women's Lives*
   (New York: Knopf, 1996), xiv–xv.

10 Excerpt from 'For Ann Gregory' by W.B. Yeats reprinted in the United States with the permission of Simon & Schuster from *The Poems of W.B. Yeats: A New Edition*, edited by Richard J. Finneran, 240. Copyright © 1933 by Macmillan Publishing Company; renewed 1961 by Bertha Georgie Yeats. Reprinted in Great Britain with the permission of A.P. Watt Ltd., London.

11 George Macaulay Trevelyan, *History of England* (London: Longmans, Green, 1926), 323.

12 Gordon S. Haight, *George Eliot & John Chapman: With Chapman's Diaries* (New Haven, CT: Yale University Press, 1940), 172.

13 Rosemary Ashton, *George Eliot: A Life* (London: Hamish Hamilton, 1996), 93.

14 Jane Harrison, *Prolegomena to the Study of Greek Religion* (New York: World, 1903; rpt. 1959).

15 Ashton, *George Eliot*, 96, 193.

16 Katharine Graham, *Personal History* (New York: Knopf, 1997), 130.

17 Elizabeth Gaskell, *Charlotte Brontë*; quoted in Helene Moglen, *Charlotte Brontë: The Self Conceived* (New York: Norton, 1976), 106.

18 Moglen, *Charlotte Brontë*, 194.

19 Wilkie Collins, *The Woman in White* (1859–60; rpt. Harmondsworth: Penguin, 1974), 58.

20 E.M. Forster, *A Passage to India*, Chapter XXIV.

CHAPTER TWO

The Evolution of the Female Memoir

Before continuing with this series of lectures, I am going to devote an interlude to the subject of sex, particularly to the distinctions between male and female sexual pleasure and the relation of these to narrative and plot. Until just the day before yesterday, all narratives and plots were modelled upon and identified with the linear pattern of male sexuality. Yale professor Peter Brooks has used the following terms to describe what he calls 'the masterplot': he speaks of 'awakening' and 'arousal' taking their course towards 'significant discharge.' You will have noticed that these words outline the pattern of male sexual performance, the recognition of which pattern Brooks believes to be essential for understanding all literature.

Male sexual action does indeed follow this pattern. It is, in fact, a ubiquitous pattern that we have come to take for granted, but is it universal in its application to narrative? Professor Susan Winnett, in a brilliant article entitled 'Women, Men, Narrative, and the Principles of Pleasure,'[1] has for the first time brought the inevitable application of this male sexual pattern to narrative into question, by introducing the equally significant rhythms of female sexuality. Is there, she asks, always the same 'master plot' imitating linear male sexuality, or do some narratives reflect female sexual experience?

Woman's sexual pleasure, she reminds us, neither begins nor ends in the same rhythm as men's. In Winnett's words, woman can begin her own arousal at whatever point she finds exciting; 'without defying the conventions dictating that sex be experienced more or less together, she can begin and end her pleasure according to' her own fantasy (507). Women may be said to have neither a path nor a linear rise and fall; rather, their sexual experience may be defined as a series of circles, a rhythm that may appear to men, and to those of us taught to think like men, unfamiliar, repetitive, and declining to proceed to a single, ordained finale.

As Winnett demonstrates, traditional criticism has assumed the universality of the male paradigm. Female narrative, on the other hand, has long been resistant to this male plot, a resistance that feminist criticism has only recently made evident. Winnett suggests, for example, that the long inability to appreciate George Eliot's *Romola* is to be explained by that novel's circular narrative pattern, so opposed to conventional conclusion. In *The Mill on the Floss*, Maggie's drowning, rather than the ending for which we long, also arises from Eliot's resistance to the 'master plot.' These novels in their narrative form defy the male pattern we have long been taught to anticipate.

I, too, resist this pattern. Therefore, it may seem to you, as I progress through these lectures, that I am repeating myself, turning back again to points apparently established earlier. Although this pattern may be unfamiliar to you, these seeming repetitions are, in fact, returns in a different mode for a new reason, and although a certain circularity will inevitably appear, it is not unintentional.

I return with two observations from contemporary feminist critics. One is the theologian Rosemary Reuther, who wrote: 'It is almost impossible for an individual alone to dissent from this culture. Alternate cultures and communities must be built up to support the dissenting consciousness.'[2]

The other is the literary critic Margaret Homans: 'While victimization takes relatively open forms with respect to race or nationality, the silencing and oppression experienced by women as women are masked as their choice.'[3] It is only recently that groups of women interested in feminism have evolved to offer support for a dissenting consciousness. At the same time, the refusal of many women to mask their common role as their choice has encouraged them to risk existing in a state of liminality, that is, in a state that is on the threshold of societal transformation. And, as I said last night, liminality is the condition of moving from one state to another under conditions which are, by definition, unstable.

The concept of liminality arose among anthropologists, and has been given particular attention in the work of Victor Turner. Victor Turner and Tom Driver's book, *Liberating Rites*, subtitled 'Our Need for Liberating Rites that Transform Our Lives & Our Communities,' are my chief sources here. Driver has approached the subject as a condition of ritual,[4] and his thesis is that ritual, which encourages the condition of liminality, is necessary to a living and changing society or religion. As he remarks, 'In their liminality, rituals exist outside many of the rules and expectations society normally imposes upon behavior. Rituals partly substitute for society's codes of behavior special codes of their own' (164).

Liminality, in Driver's words, is a 'destructuring in relation to ... the sum total of rules, norms, and statusmarkers that society keeps in place to define and govern its institutions and to control the processes of material production' (158). You may well wonder why I mention 'the processes of material production' here. Let me give you two examples. Where would the billion-dollar industry of cosmetics, fashion, plastic surgery, hair styling, and dieting be without women's eagerness to achieve some (by definition unreachable, at least for long) ideal of beauty? Second, most societies as we know them can function only if the housewife's services are offered for free.

Now the overwhelming characteristic of those in liminality, also called 'threshold people,' is, according to Turner, that they are 'necessarily ambiguous, since this condition and these persons elude or slip through the network of classifications that normally locate states and position in cultural space. Liminal entities are neither here nor there; they are betwixt and between the positions assigned and arrayed by law, custom, convention, and ceremonial' (quoted in Driver, 158). Marina Warner tells us that Joan of Arc called herself 'la Pucelle,' a word with no exact English equivalent. According to Warner, 'it means virgin, but in a special way ... It denotes a time of passage, not a permanent condition. It is a word that looks forward to a change in state.' Warner continues:

> With an instinct for seizing a central image of power, which Joan possessed to an extraordinarily developed degree, she picked a word for virginity that captured with doubled strength the magic of her state in her culture. It expressed not only the incorruption of her body, but also the dangerous border into maturity or full womanhood that she had not crossed and would not cross ... During the whole course of her brief life Joan of Arc placed herself

thus, on borders, and then attempted to dissolve them and to heal the division they delineated. In the very ambiguity of her body, which had to be shown to the crowd to assure them that she was a woman, in the name that she chose [pucelle] which means virgin and yet simultaneously captures all the risk of loss – she shows herself to span opposites, to contain irreconcilable oppositions.[5]

To contain irreconcilable oppositions is, as I shall suggest, to be a woman in a state of liminality.

From Turner's and Driver's studies of ritual, I have abstracted that concept of liminality which, I believe, best describes and evokes the significant, indeed that exact condition in which writing women both earlier and of our time have found themselves. As Driver explains,

> [u]nder patriarchy women have found it far from easy to perform themselves. To do so has often been difficult to the point of horror. A woman might rather be a madwoman in an attic, or dead on the floor, than to be a real person in public, so strong was (is) the determination of men to keep her from the ability to perform her will. Women are learning slowly and painfully to display their own truth in public, through a process of trying by increments to enact themselves. (117)

In other words, 'women turn to the experience of liminality to help them find viable alternatives to patriarchy' (165). As Turner famously announced, 'Liminality is the mother of invention' (quoted in Driver, 166).

Throughout the last two centuries, literature can stand

as evidence of that liminality – providing us with women characters always on the threshold, always 'betwixt and between.' The essence of liminality is revealed in women's experience once they are willing to move from convention to another form of self-expression. And to do this they must, of course, have conquered the two problems I have quoted to you: the difficulty of individual dissent, and the recognition that female oppression is always masked as women's choice, what women want. For despite Freud's asking of the question, he certainly thought he knew what women wanted.

In *Writing a Woman's Life* I suggested that it is easier to live certain dissents than to imagine them, and George Eliot is certainly the prime example of that. She lived far more courageously, in far more liminal a state than she allowed to any of her heroines. True, Maggie Tulliver asks why the blonde woman always triumphs and the energetic dark woman, like Maggie, is put down, but she does not, once she is an adult, wait for an answer. In *Daniel Deronda* the heroine, Gwendolen Harleth, wonders 'whether she need take a husband at all – whether she could not achieve substantiality for herself and know gratified ambition without bondage' (295).[6] Inevitably, she finds her ambition thwarted and her bondage far worse than she had bargained for. Only Daniel Deronda's mother, whom he meets once, late in the long novel, has experienced the struggle of an unconventional woman; she is genuinely talented as Gwendolen was not. 'You are not a woman,' she explains to her son, trying unsuccessfully to make him understand her life.

You may try – but you can never imagine what it is to have a man's force of genius in you, and yet to suffer the slavery of being a girl. To have a pattern cut out – this is the Jewish woman, this is what you must be; this is what you are wanted for; a woman's heart must be of such a size and no larger, else it must be pressed small, like Chinese feet; her happiness is to be made as cakes are, by fixed receipt. (694)

But lesser novelists than George Eliot – are lesser novelists, undeserving of greatness, more courageous when it comes to countering convention? – attacked the confinements of women's lives more directly, sometimes by disguise.

So Elaine Showalter suggests that the

brilliance of the Victorian novel *Lady Audley's Secret* is that [Mary E.] Braddon makes her would-be murderess the fragile blond angel of domestic realism: not Maggie Tulliver, but Lucy Deane; not Marion Halcombe but Lucy Fairlie. This dangerous woman is not the rebel or the bluestocking, but the 'pretty little girl' whose indoctrination in the female role has taught her secrecy and deceitfulness, almost as secondary sex characteristics.[7]

Braddon's use of this disguise was particularly brilliant, because the assumption is always that any woman who is challenging the prevailing myths about beauty or women's place must have failed to attract men. So Norman Mailer, appearing in a debate with Germaine Greer, said to her, 'You're better looking than I thought.' At about the same time, *Esquire* magazine defined feminism as 'a bunch of ugly women screaming at each other on television.'[8] This exact ridicule is and has long been used on any woman who dares to question the patriarchal definition of women as defined by beauty; calling feminists ugly is the best weapon to use against them. Gloria Steinem, because she was beautiful, was, as I mentioned in yesterday's lecture, an anomaly and a cause of anxiety to the media. They called her the intelligent man's pin-up and other things. No one could claim she had become a feminist because no man would have her (though I have heard even that accusation made on television), but many broadcasters told her that they could understand her better if she were a lesbian. Thus did they manage to condemn as ugly both feminists and lesbians. As Deborah Nord notes, 'throughout, Dickens signals unnaturalness in women by marking them as masculine.'[9] And if women cannot be marked as masculine, then they must be marked as old. Remember Gilbert and Sullivan's *Trial by Jury*, where the singer complains of having to marry the judge's 'elderly, ugly daughter. She could very well pass for forty-three in the dusk with a lamp behind her'?

Nor can literature really serve to counter these clichés. Even when girls read of the female desire to be individual, autonomous, a working person, the power of the culture, of what Naomi Wolf calls the 'beauty myth,' overcomes any message of strength with which literature may endow them: As Wolf puts it, 'Tales taught to children as parables for proper values become meaningless for girls as the [beauty] myth begins its work' (63). So many girls prefer Amy in *Little Women* to Jo. When the newest movie

version of *Little Women* came out in 1994, Caryn James, a
film critic for the New York Times, wrote an article for that
paper's Book Review entitled: 'Amy Had Gold Curls; Jo
Had a Rat; Who would you rather be?' Jo, of course, had
much more than a rat; among much else, she had the
talent of Louisa May Alcott. Caryn James 'admitted' (her
word) that she wanted to be Amy. Alas, despite the testi-
mony of many accomplished women that they identified
with Jo, James was far from alone.[10]

In the novels of E.M. Forster, neither Margaret in *How-
ards End* nor Adele Quested in *A Passage to India* is beautiful, to say the least, but each is courageous and willing to
transform herself. And in Virginia Woolf's last novel,
Between the Acts, she describes the plans for a pageant:
'The boys wanted the big parts; the girls wanted the fine
clothes.' Miss LaTrobe, who has written and is directing
the pageant, herself highly suspect to the villagers, being
probably foreign and probably a lesbian, understands
all too well that the boys want to be challenged in order to
be noticed; the girls want to be noticed in order to be
challenged.

As to the Bible, in the Old Testament, Jacob prefers the
more beautiful Rachel to the plainer Leah and will work
seven more years for her; in the New Testament, Jesus
prefers Mary sitting at his feet to Martha waiting on the
table. Why is it that we always have the impression that
Mary is beautiful and Martha is not?

I have returned to the discussion of the requirement of
beauty in women not only because it so clearly insists on
women as captives of conventional womanhood, but also
because the need to judge women as objects of flirtation

influences prominent women even more notably than it
does men – with harsh results for the cause of feminism.

Among those who have come to prominence in the
United States since the Second World War, there have
been few women of intellectual authority. Those that have
achieved this status can be counted on the fingers of one
hand thus: Hannah Arendt, Mary McCarthy, Susan Sontag,
Helen Vendler, Diana Trilling.These are compelling women
with eventful lives, and though they may well have each
met the others, and despite the fact that two of them were
close friends, they have one salient characteristic in common: they were all *not* feminists, indeed explicitly against
feminism. They made their reputations as honorary men,
or, in an earlier formulation, as one of the boys. There can
be no question that identification with women as a group,
or with feminism, would have risked that powerful identity, and that they knew it.

There is a corollary to this: *no feminist* since the Second
World War has achieved intellectual authority in the United
States, let alone the intellectual authority of these five
women. Women on the road to prominence have avoided
feminism with avidity in order to achieve their goal. And
the correlary of *that* is that feminists have paid more than
an obvious price for their devotion to the cause of women's
equality. Not only is their womanliness questioned, but
their cause suffers.

The way to fame and authority for a female is clear.
Marianne Moore, Louise Bogan, and Elizabeth Bishop
each achieved poetic fame and awards with a poetry
which little noted their womanhood. Moore's sex is far
from immediately evident in her poetry; Bishop refused

to be included in any anthology of women's poetry; and Bogan wrote a poem deriding women that would have been worthy of one of her misogynist male contemporaries and friends. As a critic of poets, Professor Helen Vendler has chosen since 1980 to discuss at length only two women poets, Jorie Graham and Rita Dove, neither of whom makes any poetic point of her gender – although Vendler does dwell on the importance to her poetry of Dove's 'blackness.'

It certainly appears that the explanation of all this is simple enough: were a woman sufficiently attractive and intelligent to acquire a position of apparent equality among the men of intellectual authority, she saw no reason to risk that achievement by bringing other women along with her, by helping those without her extraordinary endowments and good fortune. At the start of this women's movement, the phenomenon of the 'Queen Bee' was immediately identified: the woman who, alone among powerful men, cherished her unique status and refused to understand that other women could not as easily 'make it as she did.' When all is said and done, Queen Bees seem, three decades later, still to have monopolized the positions of female intellectual authority, however much women, thanks to feminism, have gained in other spheres. Is there a more than obvious explanation for this, or is it an indication of these women's repeated need not to refuse, at any price, the tempting welcome of powerful men?

Arendt did not, as she repeatedly asserted, care for the 'Negro question' or the 'Jewish question,' but she discussed both seriously on many occasions. The 'woman question' she simply refused to notice. This is the more surprising in that, more than with any other 'question,' those involved in the women's movement undertook reform, which she approved of, rather than revolution together with violence, which she detested. Yet women as a 'question' were beneath consideration, for Arendt and others; feminists existed only to be individually mocked. Thus, when a man complained to Hannah Arendt about Simone de Beauvoir, author of *The Second Sex* and a leading French intellectual, Arendt replied,'The trouble with you, William, is that you don't realize that she's not very bright. Instead of arguing with her, you should flirt with her.'[11]

Like these women of intellectual authority, the most famous of women memoirists, George Sand and Gertrude Stein, each saw herself as a unique female, professionally unaccompanied by any woman her equal, however many private female friendships they enjoyed. As their memoirs record, they relished their place as exceptions. The genre of autobiography – or memoir, as we now seem to call it – long defined by men, has until now not served most women as they undertake to describe the stories of their lives. Those forcefully influential early writers of male autobiography, Augustine and Rousseau, have provided us with inadequate patterns.

Before Sand and Stein and their like, women did not see themselves as exceptions but, quite the contrary, found little reason to claim sufficient justification for an autobiography. So, women writing memoirs in early centuries apologized for undertaking so unwomanly an act: Margaret Cavendish Duchess of Newcastle rhetorically asks in 1650, 'Why hath this lady writ her own life.'[12]

Nor did this note of apology change for centuries. In *Writing a Woman's Life* I speak of how women's autobiographies denied that the author had had any ambition, or control over her own career, or had suffered in any way on her road to achievement. The autobiographies of exceptional women – Golda Meir, Eleanor Roosevelt, Ida Tarbell – were written with the aim of denying their singularity: they claimed to be ordinary, womanly women plucked by chance from the usual female role. Women knew they had to choose between self-denigration, thus proving themselves women, or boasts of their accomplishments in a male world, thus proving themselves not women.

Later, those refusing the category 'women' came to write of themselves as neither women nor men. The earliest women psychoanalysts were perfect examples of this attitude, warning their women patients that the acquisition of 'male' intelligence and ambition would unsex them, render them unfit for maternity and, indeed, all femininity. These judgments did not, however, apply to the woman analyst herself, who was making such declarations. Helene Deutsch is the earliest and clearest example, but many followed; these fortunate few considered themselves to belong to some unnamed third category, which need not worry about the prescriptions applying to 'ordinary' women.

The sorts of women's memoirs being published in great numbers these days, however, are almost as characteristic of liminality as are plain women. They search for, or reflect upon, the changes in their lives they have themselves brought about, and which they see as continuing to affect them as they remain in a state of liminality. Indeed, the genre has become so popular that, as often happens in the wake of women's originality and bravery, those who wish only for celebrity and a big advance write memoirs, usually sexual and outrageous in nature, to cash in on the trend. I speak here, however, of honourable memoirs appearing in great numbers, almost all written with courage, honesty, and a certain risk.

Looking at memoirs written by women today, we are immediately struck by several other immense shifts in emphasis. In the old days, one wrote an autobiography or memoir only if one was famous; one related how that accomplishment had been achieved. Now, the most significant memoirs are being written by hitherto unknown authors, and the memoirs themselves confer fame; Maxine Hong Kingston and Maya Angelou are two who became famous through and after publishing their memoirs; there are many other examples. As Paul John Eakin has put it, the writing of autobiography has come to be not merely the 'passive, transparent record of an already completed self but rather ... [a] decisive phase of the drama of self-definition.'[13]

Women memoirists have at last found themselves at ease with that drama.

Congruent with that development, the authors of female *Bildungsroman* are getting younger; the idea of the woman subject has changed. One no longer looks back for a pattern, but writes, and looks both backward and forward in the hope of perceiving a possible pattern in advance of its having been lived. Nor is there any longer an absolute necessity to position oneself as a token women among men, or for a male to clear one's way, as with Beauvoir and Sartre. I do not believe in blaming Beauvoir for her association with or devotion to Sartre; in her day a male mentor or companion was essential; today, professionally speaking, he is less so.

Lovers, even mentors, are hardly the centrepiece of current women's memoirs. Instead, the writers of these memoirs record their threshold experiences as they encounter or, more probably, hope for a world markedly different from the one in which they grew up. So Alice Kaplan, in *French Lessons*, relates her compulsion to learn French, to exist and think in French, in order to separate herself from her early life at home.[14] This 'other' language provided her an entrance into the state of liminality – on the cusp of two cultures.

The alterations in the autobiographical subject are, not surprisingly, most readily observed in the memoirs of young women who exist between worlds: as Asian Americans, or, in England, as working-class girls enabled by changes in education following the Second World War to gain entrance into the middle class. Let us begin with these.

In 1950 Jade Snow Wong wrote *Fifth Chinese Daughter*, the story of her upbringing under, as she put it, 'the standards of Imperial China.'[15] Like Maxine Hong Kingston, the author of *The Woman Warrior*, she had to find a life between her parents' old ideals and her life as an American girl in San Francisco. Jade Snow, properly humble, speaks of herself only in the third person, and her recognition of the place of a girl in Chinese culture is presented flatly and straightforwardly. She hears one of her older sisters say to another, after the celebration of the birth of her brother, Forgiveness from Heaven: 'This joyfulness springs only from the fact that the child is at last a son, after three daughters born in the fifteen years between the son Blessing from Heaven and him. When Jade Precious Stone was born before him, the house was quiet. There was no such display.' Jade Snow realizes that if her brother was more important to Mama and Daddy than dear baby sister Precious Stone, it was because Precious Stone was only a girl. And Jade Snow herself was a girl, and thus 'unalterably less significant than the new son in their family' (27).

Much later, at a wedding, Jade Snow's mother tells her of the brutalities visited on a bride in China. Her daughter asks why they abuse the bride so. The mother answers: 'It is to prepare the bride for her new role of submission ... Her personality will be completely submerged' (144).

Fifth Chinese Daughter is an excellent account of a Chinese-American girl's accommodation to a new culture and of her eventual forgiveness of her parents. In writing of this, however, the daughter respects the old linear form of autobiography even while, ironically, she cannot use the word 'I': the Chinese word for the female 'I' is 'slave.' *The Woman Warrior*, written twenty-five years later, in 1975, is, by comparison, a new art form. Fiction has been used, not as the opposite of truth, but to capture the tension the mother embodies. Telling Maxine that 'girls are like maggots in the rice,' that 'it is more profitable to raise geese than daughters,' her mother also tells her the story of the woman warrior; she endows her daughter with the power of language, the 'talk story.' When,

Kingston writes, she heard those sayings about maggots and geese from her parents, she 'had to get out of hating range.' It is Kingston's mother who both imprisons and empowers her, and in the end withdraws. 'She said I would grow up a wife and a slave, but she taught me the song of the warrior woman. I would have to grow up a warrior woman.'[16] The new form of narrative developed in *The Woman Warrior*, the intertwining of Chinese legend and the lives of Chinese immigrants in San Francisco, embodies the conflicting and eventually empowering influence of less than properly passive mothers.

Annette Kuhn's memoir of growing up as an English working-class girl, while it also presents the struggle between the mother and daughter, is primarily a story of class, and of the shared knowledge of both mothers and daughters that the daughter, in leaving home, will enter another, utterly different social stratum. To achieve this, daughters must individuate themselves as *not like her*.

Kuhn writes about her experience as compared with memoirs of working-class men.

> The scholarship boy is not me, even if I know all about his sense of belonging nowhere. If this boy has had to renounce the vitality and toughness of the streets, he does find comfort among the women of the house as he settles to his homework on a corner of the kitchen table, taking it as read that he has no part to play in their household tasks. There is no place at this table, though, for the scholarship girl ... Here, a grown daughter surrounded by school books would be nothing short of provocation ... The scholarship girl does not belong with any of [the women in the work-

ing-class man's story]. If she wants a role in this story, the scholarship girl must, it seems, create it for herself.[17]

It is surely worth noting, that in this struggle to grasp at the new opportunities offered by education, supposedly equally to both sexes, being female is still an extra burden. Carolyn Steedman's *Landscape for a Good Woman*, which made her famous, dwells largely on the terrible alienation from her mother:'She made me believe that I understood everything about her, she made me believe that I was her; her tiredness, the pain of having me, the bleeding, the terrible headaches. She made me good because I was a spell, a piece of possible good fortune, a part of herself that she exchanged for her future: a gamble.'[18] As Adrienne Rich has taught us, daughters fear becoming their mothers.

Steedman is provocative on the refusal of women to be mothers in a world in which, until recently, women could not refuse motherhood. She quotes an item considered 'newsworthy' in England: 'Four years ago my mother informed my sisters and myself that she had no desire to see us again. She gave no particular reason except to say that she "had had enough of families" ... Other women admitted to similar experiences with their mothers' (150, n. 3).

Steedman's memoir, like Kuhn's, is also one of class; Steedman writes for others like her, outsiders whose stories have not been told, 'people in exile, the inhabitants of the long streets.' She writes, 'I was – and am – the first person in my family ever to have stayed at school beyond the compulsory leaving age.'[19] She thus speaks for those who are in exile from a society where ambitions are easily achieved and desires readily satisfied.

Steedman admits to pitching class against gender, resenting feminists with middle-class origins; the middle-class woman's move towards feminism cannot appear as dramatic to her as the move from working class to middle class. Nancy K. Miller has questioned this, since she and Steedman both 'moved' primarily against the mother:

> And yet, *Landscape for a Good Woman* moves me because of the powerful ways in which it renders the maternal legacy that makes the daughter *not* a mother. Reading as a middle-class girl now grown up, I meet this unmothered daughter through a gesture of counter-identification. Yes, our childhoods are the site of our enduring difference ... And yet, despite her warnings, against her resistance, I read with her ... along her lines, as a woman who lacked the desire to mother.(62)

Maxine's Hong Kingston's mother, working all day in the family laundry, does not want to hear a long account of her daughter's sins. Kingston writes:

> I had grown inside me a list of over two hundred things that I had to tell my mother so that she would know the true things about me and to stop the pain in my throat ... My mother's most peaceful time was in the evenings when she starched the white shirts. My father and sisters and brothers would be at their own jobs, mending, folding, packaging. Steam would be rising from the starch, the air cool at last. Yes, that would be the time and place for the

telling ... I hunkered down between the wall and the wicker
basket of shirts ...

'Mother,' I whispered and quacked.

'I can't stand this whispering,' she said ...

So I had to stop ... I had probably interrupted her in the
middle of her own quiet time when the boiler and presses
were off and the cool night flew against the windows in
moths and crickets. Very few customers came in. Starching
the shirts for the next day's pressing was probably my
mother's time to ride off with the people in her own mind
... 'Leave me alone,' she said.

What is remarkable in these recent memoirs is that the
mother is seen not only in her inadequacy as a model, but
also as the secret bestower of possibility. It is a mixed, not
to say double message, but in our time it has given girls
the chance to avoid the mother's conventionally conceived role and to create their own lives though the writing of a memoir of their lives with and against their
mothers. It is a long way from the days of 'I Remember
Mama,' with its glorification of the brave, immigrant
mother, and an even longer way from the Beauvoir/Sand
sort of memoir. There, the mother is simply disregarded
as a model, and the daughter sets out to become a son and
to take her place as a non-woman among men.

The necessity of leaving the mother, perhaps even of
making her an enemy amidst terrible guilt, has always
been a characteristic of women's memoirs, in a way very
different from the memoirs of men. Even when sons became far more educated than their fathers, even when
that education opened an abyss between the father and

son, as, for example, in Philip Roth's *Patrimony*, the father doesn't feel he has lost the son as mothers feel they have lost their daughter. For women, it is the mother who holds the secret of escape, it is the mother who holds the key to liberation. And that key is denial, an active denial, of the mother's life.

My father used to love the adage, attributed to Mark Twain, of how at fourteen he thought his father a fool, and at twenty-one he was astonished at how much the old man had learned in seven years. That is a male story. For what the modern girl of the memoir learns is not that her mother embodied a different kind of wisdom, eventually perceptible, but that the mother must herself metaphorically die to free the daughter. The mother is all the daughter does not want to be. As Shirley Lim has written: 'For many of us, it is the story of our mothers that makes a female heroic so necessary, yet also so impossible.'[20]

Nancy K. Miller has also recognized that '[l]eaving home has always been a condition, often a metaphorical one, for writing an autobiography. For women, this departure does not go easily, even at the end of the twentieth century' (94). Hence memoirs of childhood (and leaving mother) which allow one to be in two places at the same time, living now, remembering then. Miller might have added that 'leaving home' may have been a condition for autobiography for men, but it was only late in the twentieth century that it became the chief motive in the autobiographies of young women. For, as Miller observes:

> The memoirist of the 1990s writes unapologetically from her role as a player on public stages ... In itself this ...

immediately announces something historically new that refutes some of the earliest feminist claims for women's autobiography: that unlike men's, autobiography by women is turned inward toward an intimate, interior life, located in the private and domestic sphere women are said to inhabit. Here, the private and public are not opposed or even juxtaposed to each other in some simple discrete or binary way; this is a difference in vision worth observing.[21]

These new memoirists of the 1990s leave home and take their place on the public stage, but achieve public recognition only with, or after, the publication of their memoirs. As Colleen Chesterman has written, 'Only in another country can they develop themselves, can they reach fulfillment. This seems to be associated particularly with women who see themselves as intellectuals or creators.'[22]

And so the protagonists of these women's memoirs step into a state of liminality in regard both to their homes and to their mothers. These same mothers were, in almost every case, refusers of the liminal state, preferring to suffer and strive without affronting society's conventions or expectations of women. As Nancy Miller writes, 'Daughters don't forgive their mothers easily, even when as women they see how their mother's struggle with marriage plots and their own unfinished business as daughters makes them alike' (151). It does not, of course, make them identical, since one exists in a state of suffering, and the other in a state of liminality. Forgiving the mother, Miller seems to suggest, would necessitate accepting her static struggle as inevitable. It is the stasis, the failure of the mother to move out in any self-generated direction, that the daughter, whatever sympathy she may or may not feel for her mother, cannot forgive. So Jill Ker Conway writes of her mother in *The Road from Coorain*: 'I should have left her to her rage, fought her harder ... but it was too late now ... It was sad that the form her anger took was something I couldn't cope with any longer.'[23] And as Rich has written, 'The loss of the daughter to the mother, the mother to the daughter, is the essential female tragedy.'[24]

Daughters face what Alice Kaplan has called 'the sense of a past that can't be erased, but which is always incomplete' (213). Still engaged with their mother's dissatisfactions, daughter memoirists who are creators and achievers must move, have moved, between their mother's world and the one they have made for themselves, into a liminal condition which, Victor Turner tells us, eludes 'the network of classifications that normally locate states and position in cultural space.'[25] Unlike the women of intellectual authority who sought only the company of exceptional men, these new daughters seek, welcome, find support in the company of their own sex. They move in a space that has not yet been made stable or identified beyond its condition of liminality.

NOTES

1 Susan Winnett, 'Coming Unstrung: Women, Men, Narrative, and Principles of Pleasure,' *PMLA* 105/3 (May 1990): 505–18.
2 Quoted in Nancy Mairs, *Voice Lessons: On Becoming a (Woman) Writer* (Boston: Beacon, 1994), 23.
3 Ibid., 81.

4 Tom F. Driver, *Liberating Rites: Understanding the Transformative Power of Ritual* (Boulder, CO: Westview, 1997).

5 Marina Warner, *Joan of Arc: The Image of Female Heroism* (New York: Vintage, 1982), 22–3. This passage was brought to my attention in Gail B. Griffin's *Calling: Essays on the Teaching of the Mother Tongue* (Pasadena, CA: Trilogy, 1992).

6 George Eliot, *Daniel Deronda* 1876 (Harmondsworth: Penguin, 1967).

7 Elaine Showalter, *A Literature of Their Own: British Women Novelists from Brontë to Lessing* (Princeton, NJ: Princeton University Press, 1977), 165.

8 Naomi Wolf, *The Beauty Myth* (New York: Morrow, 1995), 71.

9 Deborah Epstein Nord, *Walking the Victorian Streets: Women, Representation, and the City* (Ithaca, NY: Cornell University Press, 1995), 95fn.

10 Caryn James, *New York Times Book Review*, 25 December 1994, 3.

11 *Between Friends: The Correspondence of Hannah Arendt and Mary McCarthy*, ed. and with an introduction by Carol Brightman (New York: Harcourt Brace, 1995), xiii.

12 Quoted in Mary Mason, 'The Other Voice: Autobiographies of Women Writers,' in *Autobiography: Essays Theoretical and Critical*, ed. James Olney (Princeton, NJ: Princeton University Press, 1980), 208.

13 Paul John Eakin, *Fictions in Autobiography: Studies in the Art of Self-Invention* (Princeton, NJ: Princeton University Press, 1985).

14 Alice Kaplan, *French Lessons: A Memoir* (Chicago: University of Chicago Press, 1993).

15 Jade Snow Wong, *Fifth Chinese Daughter* (1950; rpt Seattle: University of Washington Press, 1989), vii.

16 Maxine Hong Kingston, *The Warrior Woman: Memoirs of a Girlhood among Ghosts* (New York: Knopf, 1976).

17 Annette Kuhn, *Family Secrets: Acts of Memory and Imagination* (London: Verso, 1995), 102.

18 Carolyn Kay Steedman, *Landscape for a Good Woman: A Story of Two Lives* (New Brunswick, NJ: Rutgers University Press, 1987), 141.

19 Quoted in Nancy K. Miller, *Bequests and Betrayals: Memoirs of a Parent's Death* (New York: Oxford University Press, 1996), 85.

20 Shirley Geok-Lin Lim, *Among the White Moon Faces: An Asian-American Memoir of Homelands* (New York, The Feminist Press, 1996), 5.

21 Nancy K. Miller, 'Public Statements, Private Lives: Academic Memoirs for the Nineties,' *Signs* 22/4 (Summer 1997): 981–1015.

22 Quoted in ibid.

23 Jill Ker Conway, *The Road from Coorain* (New York: Knopf, 1989), 237.

24 Adrienne Rich, *Of Woman Born* (New York: Norton, 1976), 237.

25 Quoted in Anne McClintock, *Imperial Leather: Race, Gender, and Sexuality in the Colonial Contest* (New York: Routledge, 1995), 24.

CHAPTER THREE

Embracing the Paradox

M others, as I have already argued, are the single greatest problem in the stories, whether called fiction or
memoirs, that women write and have written. For most
daughters, mothers evoke what Aristotle recommended
as the ideal response to tragedy: pity and terror. That is,
pity for the mother's condition, and terror that one might
resemble her. Even if the mother is not specifically the
object of resentment, she is rarely considered able to endow the daughter with the necessary tools for realized
ambition. Mothers tend to counsel discretion and mod-
esty. And, of course, mothers exist in a no-win position,
perhaps the most pronounced no-win situation in all human experience. Almost every child prefers the father,
who returns from the outside world; who enters to break
up a tense duo; who represents freedom, adventure, and
gaiety. Is there anywhere a mother, however advanced or
devoted to a profession, who has not watched over and
guided a child day by day, only to see the father greeted
and acclaimed as the true giver of affection and attention?
He has, perhaps, spent minutes, telling a story or fixing
a toy, but that time counts heavily in the balance. Will a
mother's attentions ever be as rare and as appreciated as a
father's?

I have often wondered, when considering rich families
in the nineteenth and early twentieth centuries where
children saw their parents, together, only once a day, if the
father was still valued more highly. I suspect he was. The
parents paid equal attention, or lack of attention, but it
was the father who won the children's affection, and who
encouraged their ambitions as much as society allowed,
and perhaps a bit more. The mother, even when freed

from domestic demands, still lived in a world of dependency on men, and devotion to fashion and entertainment.

Florence Nightingale pointed out how few of the heroines of Victorian novels had mothers – 'the heroine has *generally* no family ties (almost *invariably* no mother)'[1] – to which we might add that those mothers who did exist on the peripheries of women's stories were, almost to a woman, unsatisfactory. In Jane Austen, for example, both Mrs Bennet in *Pride and Prejudice* and Mrs Dashwood in *Sense and Sensibility* leave the necessary family decisions to their eldest daughters, themselves being either dependent or misguided. None of the Brontë heroines has a mother; those George Eliot allows are ineffectual. The lack of a mother is even more evident in the romantic or Gothic popular novels of the nineteenth century.

If few heroines of novels had mothers, few women writers of past centuries and up to times just before our own *were* mothers. True, Elizabeth Barrett Browning had a son, and Colette, when she found herself with child, was told by her mother, with more accuracy than delicacy, that Colette, unintentionally pregnant, was, in her indifference, having a 'male' pregnancy. Yet what is too seldom noted is that these women who did not bear children or adopt babies did mother; they were what we might call 'surrogate mothers': Jane Austen to her nieces, George Eliot to Lewes's sons, Virginia Woolf to her nephews and nieces.

When, however, we move into the last decades of the twentieth century, the decades in which the modern women's movement enacted itself, we discover that the

earlier feminists, those I have dubbed 'my' generation –
Adrienne Rich, Maxine Kumin, Anne Sexton – as well as
the next generation – Marilyn Hacker, Linda Paxton, Alice
Ostriker – are all mothers. But many of the feminist generation now nearing or in their fifties have not had children. In writing *Of Woman Born*, Adrienne Rich for the
first time separated the idea of motherhood from the
myths, lies, and false promises that have always sur-
rounded it. Thus the choice of whether to be a mother
may have become more conscious, although certainly not
altogether so.

It is profoundly uncertain whether the decision to have
children has ever been, for women, a genuine matter of
choice. Only in recent years has a woman been able publicly to declare her decision not to be a mother; only
recently has the very question been asked and discussed
in a serious way. Have women ever actually felt free not to
have children without bearing the burden of guilt and
social censure? Such conflict, of course, thrusts women
yet again into a state of liminality.

Similarly, marriage has come more into question; its
failures are less shrouded in secrecy, its inevitablity less
taken for granted. Adrienne Rich, who had her children
before the current women's movement, wrote this poem
about marriage, 'From a Survivor,' in 1972, after the new
feminism had taken hold.

[At this point in the lecture, I read Adrienne Rich's poem.
When, however, permission was requested to print the
poem here, that permission was denied, for reasons I
deeply regret but do not comprehend. I paraphrase her

poem here, in order that what I go on to say can be understood by the reader. I do not believe poems should be paraphrased, only quoted.

Rich's poem speaks of how her marriage began as all marriages began in the fifties; she does not know why she and her husband believed that their marriage would not fail, given the forms of marriage then. They did not realize that they, like others, could not overcome the marital climate of that time. Now she can remember his body, of what it was capable and of what it was not capable. The year after she is writing the poem would have been their twentieth anniversary, but her husband has committed suicide; perhaps they might have transformed their marriage, as they had, too late, spoken of doing. Now, she must live not with a sudden change, but with a series of short, astonishing changes, and each small transmutation will make the next one possible.

This synopsis, while giving some idea of what the poem 'says,' can in no way substitute for it. I urge the reader to search it out in Rich's volume of collected poems. My point in quoting it was to suggest, in contrast to the lovely poem that follows, the difference between a feminist poem in which the poet speaks of her willingness to dwell on a series of new thresholds, and a poem which recalls a conventional marriage which the poet can remember but cannot, within the poem, understand the cause of her misery, or her reason for recounting it.]

I want to read next a provocative poem by a woman who, like many women before her, is questioning her life without questioning the institutions that sustained that life or that had to be transformed for women to find their place in that life; a poem, that is, by a woman poet who is not a feminist. Called 'Where Did I Leave Off?' this poem is by Virginia Hamilton Adair. I offer it in comparison for its theme, not the quality of its poetry, which is excellent. Both these women poets survived husbands who suddenly and wholly unexpectedly took their own lives.

Where did I leave off yesterday?
I stood at midnight with the mouse
caught in a cornflake box and rustling slightly.
What to do next? I stepped outside
into the backdoor tangle of thorns and roses.
I did not know my neighbors.
They'd be puzzled to see a cereal box
in their backyard. Good luck,
little mouse, I said, as the box sailed
over the high fence.

Our next mouse crept
into an empty cider jug for the sweet dreg.
I stood the bottle up, a sad, sweet jail.
Almost at once she gave birth to a litter of six.
I carried the bottle of mice to Lincoln Park
and left the jug on its side, for easy exit,
under a sheltering bush. They were all
Beatrix Potter mice, dainty and lovable;
not the gross travesties of Disney.

        I was lonely
with my husband away all day at work.
But after a wild party Kentucky Derby Day,

we too began to breed in Rapley Caves, under our thicket of
      pipes
but not in a cereal box or cider bottle.

In the first cyclone to hit the eastern mid-Atlantic coast,
we moved to New Haven in such a deluge
that canoes passed us on the Boston Post Road,
and driving into New Haven,
all the elms blew down behind us.
I survived a surfeit of tainted oysters
and gave birth to our first child.
He will be 55 next week.

Why am I telling you all this?[2]

In the last decades, writing women have almost entirely determined either to re-examine old habits and loy-
alties, or to move into a different world, into an as yet
unscripted life. But we still have the old forms of family,
marriage, parenting, children, solitude, ageing, as well as
the old forms of our professions, to cope with. Into these
forms we have tried to fit new ideas, and literature is the
evidence of that tenuous liminality – that condition where
we are always on the threshold, always in between, never
accepting the old or quite succeeding in establishing the
new. I have found that only poetry is able to work new
ideas into old forms, as Adrienne Rich in the example I
read you, and many other poets have been able to do.
That is, these poets write of a liminal condition – 'a suc-
cession of brief, amazing moments' – but find earlier
forms more ready to their needs.

With memoirs the situation is quite the other way. In writing of how they find themselves between worlds, or launched into new, unfamiliar experiences, women memoirists today must invent, or create a new form. Thus, as I have suggested, they discover themselves in writing, they reach fame in writing, they re-create themselves in writing. They conclude, neither with the assurance of male autobiography nor the apologetic denial of traditional female autobiography, but with a new admission, indeed a claim, of intention, ambition, and the suffering involved. And unlike such women as Mary McCarthy and Hannah Arendt, they do not indulge in what might be called 'magisterial intellectualism.'

Deborah Epstein Nord's account of Beatrice Webb's memoir, *My Apprenticeship*, revised and published in 1926 when Webb was sixty-eight, suggests how the form of women's memoirs and autobiographies had by then evolved. As Nord puts it, '[a] general pattern of de-conversion and subsequent rebirth characterizes the genre of autobiography to which *My Apprenticeship* belongs. The autobiographer describes a loss of orthodox faith, a period of crisis, of acute despair and dejection, when the old faith is found to be inadequate; a search for new faith to fill the void of unbelief; and a rebirth in newfound faith and vocation.'[3]

This form, widely used by men in the nineteenth century, has been called a 'conversion narrative.' Faith was what one could lose, its loss was traumatic and deeply significant, and something had to be found to replace it; that something was usually seen as a vocation, a calling to work that is not only all-consuming but that can be seen to be undertaken with a kind of religious dedication. Beatrice Webb's, Nord tell us, 'was the first British woman's autobiography to take the classic Victorian form of spiritual crisis and conversion. Like Mill and Carlyle, she wrote of the search for faith and vocation, of the need for belief and work. Like them she considered her work to be emblematic of her life, and regarded her own spiritual and intellectual development as the essence of her existence' (13–14).

Like Beatrice Webb's, the memoirs of Jane Addams and Florence Nightingale are cries of intellectual hunger, a longing for a place to put one's life, to use one's talents, to operate in the world and not just in a meaningless daily routine of social obligations and domestic duties. Nord writes that

> Jane Addams, ill and depressed ... first observed the squalor of an urban slum from the top of a double-decker bus in London's East End while on a European trip recommended by her physician. At this sight, she wrote in *Twenty Years at Hull House*, she was seized with 'despair and resentment' and was further dismayed to realize that the only context out of which she could respond to this disquieting reality was a literary one. We women, Addams thought, waste our time 'lumbering our minds with literature,' instead of seeking contact with the real. When, after a second visit to London a few years later, she resolved to begin a settlement house in Chicago, it was as much for the sake of young, middle-class women as for that of the poor: she wanted a place 'in which young women who had been given over to study might restore a balance of activity ... and learn of life from life itself. (68)

Florence Nightingale had similar regrets and aspirations, as she reported in *Cassandra*, her account of her desperately vacuous youth that was not published during her lifetime, but first appeared in the 1920s: 'Why have women passion, intellect, moral activity – these three – and a place in society where none of the three can be exercised' (25).

Although Webb had not read Florence Nightingale, her 'religious strivings expressed ... the need for a place of usefullness in the world, and a desire for an active show of aspiration' (Nord, 92). It is clear that the literary models available to Webb were mostly by men. This meant that for Webb, as 'for most nineteenth-century women of ambition and achievement, the resolution of struggle and the satisfactory discovery of sexual and spiritual identity remained painfully elusive and, therefore, virtually impossible to describe.' Furthermore, '[i]t was as necessary to the Victorian woman's survival to keep an inner life of conflict masked as it was to keep illegitimate aspirations hidden. The writing of autobiography was, like the expression of ambition or private struggle, prohibited: both demanded an impermissible form of attention for the female self' (59).

For the women of Webb's generation, and almost up until the current feminist movement, the private and public spheres were absolutely separate, and it was impossible to reconcile them. Thus women who chose the 'public' life did not marry, and refused even to consider the married life; for those who married it was, of course, exactly the opposite. In combining them both (although she had no children), Webb was ahead of her time.

The feminist memoirs of our own time, written by

women at the cusp of fifty, or already in their fifties, are quite different. All those whose memoirs I shall discuss here are married, although the marriage plays a remarkably minor role in their memoirs. These women now write of work and of the choices they are now able to make. They are searching for new forms and new activities by which to transform the professional conditions under which they operate. They are considering how they reached the point of professional distinction that they occupy at the moment of writing.

Here we must again particularly note those writing memoirs of growing up 'betwixt and between' – those, that is, coming from a world that could not, because of class, immigration, or cultural differences, altogether prepare them for the adult and professional conditions of their lives. And, within this group, a profound distinction between the memoirs of contemporary American and British women must be mentioned.

In North America, memoirs of women born during or after the Second World War are about cultural difference, whether they are of Asian, as in the examples I have offered, or of African, Hispanic, Jewish, or European descent. They may express a sense of loss, of traditions either neglected or too assiduously observed, but they do not carry with them, or at least express with vehemence, that particular hostility against society and its class arrangements which characterizes British memoirs. We have heard Annette Kuhn's description of how hard it was for a scholarship girl, unlike a scholarship boy, to study in the kitchen of her working-class home. Carolyn Steedman, recalling her girlhood, finds herself even angrier. A social worker had come to inspect her mother's house when her mother was pregnant with her second baby, and with, we may suppose, a sneer she announced that 'this house isn't fit for a baby.' Of this bitter memory Steedman writes: 'I will do everything and anything until the end of my days to stop anyone ever talking to me like that woman talked to my mother. It is in this place, this bare, curtainless bedroom that lies my secret and shameful defiance. I read such a woman's book, meet such a woman at a party (a woman now, like me) and think quite deliberately as we talk: we are divided: a hundred years ago I'd have been cleaning your shoes. I know this and you don't.'[4]

That bitter anger, that ancient resentment, is not present in memoirs of American white women, though the animosity inspired by class or race strongly permeates the autobiographies of American black men and women. Those memoirs are, of course, liminal in a special way. Steedman can say 'a woman now, like me,' while an African-American academic, speaking of her white colleague, knows that their racial difference means, not only that this woman is *not* like her, but that she can never be like her, never know what she has known.

Unique, perhaps, to the memoirs of educated North American women is an acute concern with their professional lives. Three recent academic memoirs, which I shall be discussing, were all written by four professors at Duke University who worked together on them – reading, criticizing, encouraging each other's efforts. (Cathy Davidson, whose memoir,*Thirty-Six Views of Mount Fuji*, I discussed in my first lecture, was the fourth member of this writing group. In her memoir, you will remember, she recounts

her tenuous position between two societies, those of
Japan and the United States, to which she felt she be-
longed, cultures so different from each other that to feel at
home in each is not unlike taking regular part in a ritual or
festive occasion of sharply differentiated role playing. I
characterized her situation as one of liminality.)

These memoirs, in alphabetical order, are by Alice
Kaplan, Jane Tompkins, and Marianna De Marco Torgovnick. Each of these last names is, incidentally, a married
name, although not always the name of the man to whom
they are currently married. (Let me pause here to make a
quite irrelevant and yet to me significant point about the
liminality of current professional female nomenclature. I
am familiar with or have heard of many women, well
known, perhaps even famous, who operate under the
name of a former, usually first, husband. This seems to
me a state of liminality in no way desirable. During all
the years I taught, I urged my students, upon the acquisition of a graduate degree, to claim a name that would
be theirs for the rest of their professional lives, either a
birth name, or an adopted name. Nancy K. Miller is a
good example of the intelligent way to deal with this.
She decided, upon entering her professional life, to adopt
her mother's birth name as her own, retaining her father's
name as the middle initial. Other women make up a
name. But, the marital statistics being what they are,
changing one's professional name to one's husband's is
an impractical operation. Few listened to me then, and
few will listen now.)

These women, like all of us who begin with small questions, inevitably go on to larger and larger ones: they

question the ways in which they were taught to teach and relate to students; they question how they had been, as women, expected to encounter and present the literature they were teaching. Although they tell us something of their childhoods, it is now their professional selves that are the centre of their memoirs. Simone de Beauvoir said, expressing disappointment with the new flow of female memoirs, 'Very often women think that all they need to do is to tell ... the story of an unhappy childhood.'[5] These writers, however, are re-creating themselves even as they write; they are not only retelling the past. À la Recherche du temps perdu was all very well for Proust, but it is not the stuff of the new feminist memoir.

Alice Kaplan's memoir is entitled *French Lessons*[6] and is an account of how she determined to learn and to perfect her skills in that language as a way of developing an alternate personality. She attended a French-language school in Switzerland, and went on to take a graduate degree in French at Yale. Kaplan is Jewish, a fact which almost certainly affected her choice of dissertation subject. And here I must again digress. The whole question of being Jewish these days is, in itself, for obvious reasons, a study of liminality. There are religious Jewish women who have tried to live with, reform, or abandon the practice of Judaism, and there are Jews who accept that category as a fact of life rather than a matter of deep pride or devotion. The change in this most liminal of conditions is the result of the Holocaust, and the sense every formerly assimilated Jew must have that one is marked in a way that is unavoidable and might as well be accepted with grace. Hannah Arendt commented in this connection that she did 'not love the Jews, nor do I believe in them; I merely belong to them as a matter of course, beyond dispute and argument.'[7] I make this digression because, while Kaplan was born Jewish, and Torgovnick married a Jew, Jewishness can be said to have been a necessary but not sufficient explanation of their entrance into their professional lives.

During Kaplan's junior year abroad in France, she became fascinated by Céline's *Journey to the End of Night*. She was drawn to Céline, she tells us, by his language, but soon learned that he had come 'under the grip of a mad anti-Semitism in the 1930s, claiming his writing style was the expression of his pure French blood' (106). By the end of the German occupation, Céline was reviled in France, where he was linked to the French treatment of Jews by the Vichy government. The French Jews had been stripped 'of their professions and business and rights, forced to wear yellow stars on their coats,' and deported to die in German and Polish camps; only 3 per cent of the 76,000 French Jews sent to camps survived. Céline fled France to Germany after the war and lived out his life in exile. He inspired in Kaplan a profound and unchanging interest, perhaps even fascination, with the Fascists in France during the period of Nazi dominion.

When Kaplan was at Yale, Paul de Man headed a school of criticism so abstruse and difficult that one emerged either as a genius or having decided to drive a cab instead. (For example, de Man was, Kaplan reports, 'working on the rhetorical figure known as "catechresis"; it was the key to the whole way we students tried to think about language.' A figure of speech, Kaplan explains, is usually a substitute for the 'real,' as in metaphor. With catechresis, certain words borrow their meaning from another realm, as in the leaf of a book, the leg of a table [149–50]. I have been able to discover no other examples, and it has always seemed to me that one of the chief advantages of retiring was that I would never have to think about catechresis again. Anyway, you get an idea about the arcane quality of de Man's ideas.)

De Man died in 1984, and what Kaplan calls 'ugly scandal-mongering' followed: de Man had written that 'if French Jewish novelists were sent to a Jewish colony, the literary life of Europe wouldn't suffer' (167). He had expressed other fascist opinions, and his disgrace seemed to bring down with it the by then almost universal academic adulation of theory, or at least the use of words that one had to keep looking up because their usefulness lay in their being obscure, and in identifying their user as someone in the know. Kaplan did not take sides on the de Man issue, but there is no doubt that the revelation of his past fascism did a great deal for her reputation.

A subject that had seemed inappropriate suddenly was on target. This is an excellent example of where women could go, given the chance, and Kaplan, who had learned from feminism to be more open about herself, was able to recognize that 'de Man would have been a better teacher if he had given more of his game away ... The root of de Man's intellectual questions was in his own experience and pain' (172–3). Kaplan did not feel de Man had failed her, because she had never talked to him, had only attended his lectures. She had not tried to talk to him, because he seemed 'the least interested of anyone on the faculty' in her topic (174). What a waste, she was to think, and how much light he might have cast on her work. Behind de Man's high rhetorical stance there probably lay the eternal insistence on the part of male scholars to retain a master language.

Jane Tompkins's book *A Life in School*[8] recapitulates her own experience as a student from her childhood on, and then documents her efforts to change the manner of teaching in colleges. Rather than plan her classes in an attempt to demonstrate how much she knows of the literary subject under discussion, she works to turn the classes into a more open environment where the students can develop their own skills and learn more about themselves. She also plans excursions of various sorts with her classes, attempting to encourage bonding among the students, and between her and the students. Whether or not her attempts are considered successful will differ with each reader. The important element in her book from my point of view is that, in challenging and attempting to change the pedagogical routine, she places herself outside any institutional configuration, virtually leaping into a liminal state in which, even at the book's close, she rests unsteadily and uncertainly.

Inevitably, she experiences the loneliness that such a position in regard to societal institutions induces: 'I'd realized that for much of my life an underlying fear of loneliness had spurred me to meet standards I imagined were necessary in order to win acceptance and approval, and thus to draw to me the company of other people' (182).

Yet Tompkins, perhaps as a result of how lonely her life had been, came to understand the omission of women writers and readers from the literary canon and coura-geously worked to change this. The whole question of the canon has become, particularly in the hands of the funda-mentalist right wing in the United States, utterly distorted and misrepresented; far too much power and success have been credited to those who attempted to introduce some gender (or racial) variety into the readings of the canon. But the courage to question what had been as-sumed to be neutral, eternal, and perfect was great in-deed.

As Tompkins writes, '[m]eanwhile I went on teaching literature as though men and women writers, unlike men and women professors, had always been treated equally. It was six more years before I realized that I had been reading, writing about, and teaching a literary canon that had been determined exclusively by, and in the interests of, men' (98). Inevitably, the effect upon her of reading *Uncle Tom's Cabin* for the first time was profound:

> When I read that book and felt its amazing power, I knew something had been wrong with my literary education, something not accidental or superficial but systemic and deep. This was unquestionably one of the greatest books I had ever read ... But not once in all my years of schooling had anyone ever suggested that this book was worth read-ing; on the contrary, when Stowe's novel was mentioned, which was seldom, it was in a dismissive or condescend-ing way.
> There and then I decided to fight for that book. (106–7)

Tompkins is an Americanist, and it is Melville whose work has most continuously engaged her. But her recog-

nition of how women are rendered invisible both as professors and as writers was a clear, feminist recognition,
now to be enacted beyond her girlhood and the limita-
tions of that time.

Marianna De Marco Torgovnick, in *Crossing Ocean
Parkway*[9] is the most explicit about how being both female
and raised in a working class Italian-American family
affected her educational experiences. For example, each
of these three Duke professors is aware of the struggle
to get tenure, but only Torgovnick's mother understands
her daughter's achievement of tenure in a working-class
context:

> 'What does that mean?' my mother said when she heard
> the news. Then she reached back into her experiences as a
> garment worker, subject to seasonal 'layoffs': 'Does it mean
> they can't fire you just for nothing and can't lay you off?'
> When I said that was exactly what it means, she said: 'Very
> good. Congratulations. *That's wonderful.*' I was free from
> the bosses and from the network of petty anxieties that
> formed, in large part, her very existence. (10)

Torgovnick recalls how, at her confirmation, she was
given a new name, but that the renaming did not fool her.
She saw that the more adult female apparel the girls wore
for confirmation was the same 'ball and chain of womanhood ... I wanted to be done with that kind of femininity,
that kind of conformity. With confirmation behind me, I
was ready to make my move.' Later, she had had to fight,
on entering high school, to be allowed into the academic
track, into which the Jewish children were all directed,

while the Italian girls were expected to follow a secretarial course.

(To the importance of her Italian-American culture in Marianna Torgovnick's life can be added her impressive explanation for the violent anti-feminism of Camille Paglia. As Torgovnick explains it, Paglia internalized the Italian-American male's view of women and adopted it as her own. Explaining women who call themselves feminist and trash their sister feminists brutally and continuously is an intriguing occupation. Torgovnick's explanation is one of the most satisfactory.)

As Ann Snitow has brilliantly set forth in her essay 'A Gender Diary,' there remains within feminism an unresolved debate over the definition of a woman. One side, often identified with American feminism, believes that women have more in common with men than not, and must be considered first as human beings. The other side, called the 'essentialists' and often identified with French feminism, believes that there is something unique to womanhood – that women are not only, because of their ability to bear children, different, but also that they approach life from a wholly different standpoint.

Feminists have often been urged to 'embrace the paradox,' and, Snitow observes, this 'is just what feminism cannot choose but do. There is no transcendence, no third course. The urgent contradiction women constantly experience between the pressure to be a woman and the pressure not to be one ... cannot be dissolved through thought alone.' Snitow does suggest, however, that it may eventually and inevitably be resolved by a 'historical process.'[10] Snitow begins her article with the following autobiographical anecdote, which perfectly illustrates this paradox:

> In the early days of this wave of the women's movement, I sat in a weekly consciousness raising group with my friend A. We compared notes recently. What did you think was happening? How did you think our own lives were going to change? A said she had felt, 'Now I can be a woman; it's no longer so humiliating. I can stop fantasizing that secretly I am a man, as I used to, before I had children. Now I can value what was once my shame.' Her answer amazed me. Sitting in the same meetings during those years, my thoughts were roughly the reverse. 'Now I don't have to be a woman anymore. I need never become a mother. Being a woman has always been humiliating, but I used to assume there was no exit. Now the very idea "woman" is up for grabs. "Woman" is my slave name; feminism will give me freedom to see some other identity altogether.' (9)

It is worth noting that none of the Duke women grapples with this conflict; it does not even seem to occur to any of them.

Nor, of course, has any of them revealed any troubles that questions about their 'beauty' might have caused them, or whether or not they were, as they all evidently were, sufficiently attractive to men. Unlike George Eliot, the Duke women and their peers live at a time when women are perceived as free to choose their way of life, and where, although the acquisition of a man is, as ever, desirable to most women, it is not essential to professional women. Their beauty, or lack of it, therefore, while perhaps personally consequential, is no longer of soul-wrenching significance.

What is significant is how these memoirs demonstrate that women in this time of feminism have moved into professional areas not open to their mothers or to women of earlier generations, and how they have had to grapple with questions both new and imperious. They are undergoing the 'historical process' that Snitow recognized as the only inevitable solution to the otherwise unresolvable conflict between existentialism and equality feminism. Undergoing this process is itself the very essence of liminality.

NOTES

1 Florence Nightingale, *Cassandra* (New York: The Feminist Press, 1997), 28.

2 'Where Did I Leave Off?' from *Ants on the Melon* by Virginia Hamilton Adair, 105–6. Copyright © 1996 by Virginia Hamilton Adair. Reprinted by permission of Random House, Inc.

3 Deborah Epstein Nord, *The Apprenticeship of Beatrice Webb* (Amherst: University of Massachusetts Press, 1985), 20.

4 Carolyn Kay Steedman, *Landscape for a Good Woman: A Story of Two Lives* (New Brunswick, NJ: Rutgers University Press, 1987), 2.

5 Hélène V. Wenzel, 'Interview with Simone de Beauvoir,' *Yale French Studies no. 72: Simone de Beauvoir: Witness to a Century* 1986: 9.

6 Alice Kaplan, *French Lessons: A Memoir* (Chicago: University of Chicago Press, 1993).

7 Elisabeth Young-Buehl, *Hannah Arendt: For Love of the World* (New Haven, CT: Yale University Press, 1982), 333.

8 Jane Tompkins, *A Life in School* (New York: Addison-Wesley, 1996).

9 Marianna De Marco Torgovnick, *Crossing Ocean Parkway* (Chicago: University of Chicago Press, 1994).

10 Ann Snitow, 'A Gender Diary,' in *Conflicts in Feminism*, ed. Marianne Hirsch and Evelyn Fox Keller (New York: Routledge, 1990), 21.

CHAPTER FOUR

The Rewards of Liminality

Ann Snitow, in her essay from which I read the other day, an essay written with a rare mixture of profundity and clarity, sets forth the problem that many women of the generation now writing memoirs – women, that is to say, on either side of fifty and professionally established – face regarding their mothers.

> So entirely was I trapped in negative feelings about what women are and can do that I had repressed any knowledge of femaleness as a defining characteristic of my being. I can see now that women like me come to feminist conclusions much like my own. But this is later knowledge. My feminism came from the suburbs, where I knew no white, middle-class woman with children who had a job or any major activities outside the family. Yet, though a girl, I was promised education, offered the pretense of gender neutrality ... This island of illusions was a small world ... it is this world I return to in thought. During the day, it was safe, carefully limited, and female. The idea that this was all made me frantic ... My gifted mother taught me not the riches of home but the necessity of feminism. Feminism was her conscious as well as unconscious gift.[1]

Snitow had observed that 'some of us early [feminists] were too afraid of the lives of our mothers to recognize ourselves in them. But I remember that this throwing off of the mother's life felt like the only way to begin' (32).

As it happens, that is my story exactly. I, too, saw my mother as gifted and utterly frustrated in the hollowness of her life. More consciously, perhaps, than Snitow's mother, she taught me the necessity of feminism, although neither of us, twenty years before Snitow's girlhood, had even heard of the term. As Snitow describes the paradox, '[a] common divide keeps forming in both feminist thought and action between the need to build the identity "woman" and give it solid political meaning, and the need to tear down the very category "woman" and dismantle its all too solid history ... This tension – between needing to act as women and needing an identity not overdetermined by our gender – is as old as western feminism, it is at the core of what feminism is' (9). This tension she describes is the place of liminality.

In my lecture last night I remarked that mothers are the single greatest problem in women's memoirs and stories, however these writings are characterized. You will, of course, have noticed that I then went on to discuss in some detail three memoirs by Duke professors in which their mothers were clearly not perceived as the greatest problem. That is, these writers neither blame their mothers nor identify them as the enemy. I believe, however, that it has always been the mother who stands behind each woman as the major force in her life. It is, I would argue, the inadequacy of the mother's life that whets the daughter's appetite for achievement and, eventually, for the strength to fight even against the institution that endows her with professional status. Kaplan's work on Céline and de Man may seem an exception here. Her father died when she was young; he had been involved in the Nuremberg trials; and, in studying fascists, she was certainly, in some way, carrying on his work. Yet would the father's work, even if he died young and was in some way his daughter's chief support and inspiration, have loomed so large had the mother who remained been as riveting a role model? The absence of the mother as a model of the sort of life these women chose to live is, however negatively forceful, a vital, perhaps the vital, element in these women's lives.

Nancy K. Miller is a good example here. Her mother was everything against which Miller fought, and her recognition of both her mother's ambitions and her necessity for compromise with a less than compelling husband in no way mitigates Miller's refusal of reconciliation with that unsatisfactory parent. My conclusion is that no matter what the feminist daughter's recollections, no matter whether she lovingly forgives and cherishes the mother, whether she reconstitutes her with new understanding and compassion, whether she continues to revolt against her, even in memory, the fact is that, as Rich has said, '[t]he quality of the mother's life ... is her primary bequest to her daughter.'[2]

Yet this is true, I would claim, only of white women of whatever class. The stories of African-American women are quite different. In their stories, mothers are recollected as competent, hard-working women who do actually guide and control their families, whether a man is present or not. African-American women almost unanimously speak of their mothers with undiluted respect. Many African-American men, furthermore, attribute their accomplishments, and particularly the strength to pursue those accomplishments in the face of much adverse peer pressure, to their mothers.

Neither Steedman, who was not at her mother's deathbed, nor Miller, who was, discovered new compassion towards her dying mother. Simone de Beauvoir and Philip Roth, on the other hand, though both childless, each watched their parent, Beauvoir's mother and Roth's father, become the object of long-forgotten tenderness as they were nearing death. Roth writes:

> The next day, when Lil phoned from Elizabeth to ask how he was doing, I overheard him saying to her, 'Philip is like a mother to me.'
>
> I was surprised. I would have thought he'd say, 'like a father to me,' but his description was, in fact, more discriminating than my commonplace expectations while at the same time much more flagrant, unblinking, and enviably, unself-consciously blunt.[3]

And Beauvoir writes:

> I had grown very fond of this dying woman. As we talked in the half-darkness I assuaged an old unhappiness; I was renewing the dialogue that had been broken off during my adolescence and that our differences and our likenesses had never allowed us to take up again. And the early tenderness that I had thought dead forever came to life again, since it had become possible for it to slip into simple words and actions.[4]

I have done a certain amount of counting, admittedly the sort of statistics described cynically by statisticians as 'Aunt Agatha and me,' and this counting has reconfirmed my impression that the majority of feminists born after the Second World War, that is, women who have openly written as feminists, do not have children. As Steedman and Miller both suggest, this childlessness may arise out of a desire *not* to reproduce the maternal bond with a child of their own. This I certainly found, in writing her biography, to be true of Gloria Steinem. The sad fact is that women who refuse motherhood have often either seen themselves in actual combat with their mothers, or view their continuing relations with their mothers as a kind of warfare, and unresolved warfare at that. They see the maternal struggles as hardly worthy of replication.

The great paradox of whether or not to choose maternity, the paradox in which women live and have their being, may only become less of one when feminism takes hold: when there is more equal nurturing by fathers and mothers; when both parents bring the excitement of the outside world into the home; above all, when countries, even those not as rich as the United States, provide adequate day care and schooling.

One of the aspects, Cathy Davidson tells us in *Thirty-Six Views of Mount Fuji*, that she learned to love about Japan was 'its freedom from the classic Western notion that a person is a stable, unchanging, continuous entity, some essential self.' In Japan, 'behavior and even personality depend partly on context, on the rules of a given situation ... My Japanese self realizes that some things aren't explicable, aren't reducible to those things that, in the West, we like to partition off as "logic" or "common sense"' (101–2). What Davidson learned is that not knowing the rules added 'intensity and suspense to the simplest interaction' (90). What Davidson's 'Japanese self' came to realize is what many women since the dawn of this feminist movement have gradually come to understand: that they are expected, as Daniel Deronda's mother was expected, to follow the logical or common-sense life for a woman: dating, marriage, childbirth, mother. In my view, the reason why these old structures so appeal to some people is precisely that they can, in following them, avoid liminality, avoid hovering on the threshold, avoid having to take brave decisions and then having to live with the anxiety and uncertainty those decisions inevitably produce. It is easier to do what is expected of you than to live in 'intensity and suspense.'

Which brings me again to marriage. The point about literature in English, and especially the novel, from its earliest days to now, is that for the most part marriage ends it, whether it is Pamela's or Tom Jones's marriage, whether in the work of Jane Austen, Thackeray, or Joyce.

We have already seen how marriage is differently reflected in the poems of two women almost twenty years apart in age and further separated by the modern women's movement. As Dalma Heyn observes in her recent book *Marriage Shock*, '[t]here is a difference between that which women know, and that which the culture is willing to hear, particularly when it concerns something as treasured as marriage.'[5] Heyn quotes some intriguing statistics. Despite later marriages, and motherhood without marriage, 'over 90 percent of all American women will marry before the age of twenty-seven. Sixty-five percent of these marriages will end in divorce, but three-quarters of those ex-partners will marry again within four years' (xi–xii). However clear the failure of marriage in our time to succeed notably as an institution, the faith of most of us in it refuses to be compromised. Second marriages are, as Samuel Johnson said, the triumph of hope over experience.

Writers, to the contrary, began openly to express doubts about marriage shortly after Joyce published *Ulysses*. In Woolf's *To the Lighthouse*, Charles Tansley sits at the dinner table, wanting someone to give him a chance to expound. Sitting opposite him, Lily Briscoe, the artist, understands this:

> There is a code of behavior, she knew, whose seventh article (it may be) says that on occasions of this sort it behooves the woman, whatever her own occupation may be, to go to the help of the young man opposite so that he may expose and relieve the thigh bones, the ribs, of his vanity, of his urgent desire to assert himself; as indeed it is their duty, she reflected, in her old maidenly fairness, to help us, suppose the Tube were to burst into flames. Then, she thought, I should certainly expect Mr. Tansley to get me out. But how would it be, she thought, if neither of us did either of these things?[6]

It is this question, among others, the modern novel and the modern play begin to ask.

Writing in 1880 his second novel, which, like his first, 'nobody would publish,' Shaw not only titled his book about marriage *The Irrational Knot*, but portrayed the institution for what it was: a matter of woman-purchase. Susannah refuses to marry the man with whom she is living:

I can support myself, and maybe shew Bob a clean pair of
heels tomorrow if I choose ... I confess I shouldn't like to
make a regular legal bargain of going to live with a man. I
don't care to make love a matter of money; it gives it a taste
of the harem, or even worse. Poor Bob, meaning to be
honorable, offered to buy me in the regular way at St.
George's, Hanover Square, before we came to live here;
but, of course, I refused, as any decent woman in my
circumstances would.[7]

Shaw was ahead of his time, but not by much. In his
1908 play *Getting Married*, the bride-to-be reads the marriage service, is shocked, and almost refuses to go through
with the ceremony. In 1918, when Robert Graves married
a young woman who was kept in a continuous state of
anger by the attitude of the Huntingdon farmers to their
wives and daughters, nature followed art: 'Nancy had
read the marriage service for the first time that morning,
and been so disgusted that she all but refused to go
through with the wedding, though I had arranged for the
ceremony to be modified and reduced to the shortest
possible form.'[8]

Even earlier literary marriage was not really presented
but was accepted, like death, as one of the unavoidable
conditions of living. Where we do see it in those years in
literature, marriage appears to be a situation like war, as
Auden tells us, calling for 'patience, foresight, manoeuvre.' Only occasionally is there a glimpse of marriage
which seems to hold the promise of life. In these marriages – the Buckets in *Bleak House* and, in *Persuasion*, that
uniquely happily married couple in all Austen, the Crofts,

the woman is noted for being unusually competent for sharing to a rare degree her husband's life, decisions, and adventures, and for being openly admired by him. What we notice here, of course, is that these marriages, like that of Eliot and Lewes, bear the marks of friendship.

Oddly enough, the only extended view of a marriage in literature which can be said to a union, not of equals but of comrades, is between men: Holmes and Watson. If we observe them in their adventures and their domestic life, we discover their relationship to be in accord with tradition to the extent that the husband, Holmes, is the unquestioned leader in all their doings; but at least Watson is companion rather than an appendage or a domestic convenience. Commentators have often noted Watson's almost archetypal necessity to the detective story, but few have found his function also to be in the domestic comforts he offers Holmes – comforts, furthermore, which do not entail a large family and chinz on all the furniture.[9]

If we look to literature today for clues as to how marriage might be faced, we find that, not surprisingly, we do best by turning to popular literature, a genre growing as a result of the admiration and appreciation that has accrued to it; there are now many courses in popular literature in universities in the United States, and whole presses devoted to the publication of criticism of this genre. If the detective novel, for example, required two males, Holmes and Watson, to represent a possibly viable marriage, contemporary detective fiction, like contemporary memoirs, either ignores marriage or transforms it.

Let me insert a personal note here. When in 1964 I published, under the name of Amanda Cross, my first detective novel, there were no American women detectives in print. The only other woman detective on the shelves of the first mystery book store in New York and, I think, the whole United States, was Agatha Christie's Miss Marple. I remember fervently wishing for colleagues for my woman detective, and of all the wishes I have had since the beginning of this feminist wave, that is the only one that has been granted in full. Women detectives are past counting. Many of them are professionals, only a few, like my detective, are amateurs. They are lawyers, medical examiners, judges, police persons, government agents, and so on. But few, very few, are married. They mostly have lovers, and, if they are married, the marriages are remarkably equal, though, unlike Holmes and Watson, without subordination of either person in the partnership, and with the brains equally divided with a slight advantage on the side of the woman detective, who is, after all, the protagonist. We must, note however, that Laurie R. King, in a series of brilliant new detective novels, allies Holmes with a young woman as skilled as he in the following of clues and equally brave, whom, in the latest novel, he has married. Mrs Hudson continues as the domestic angel to these two, as she was to Holmes and Watson. This marriage and professional partnership is in sharp contrast to the marriage of Dorothy Sayers's Lord Peter Wimsey and Harriet Vane. When these two marry, Harriet entirely disappears into the roles of wife and mother and is never seen as her true self again. In contemporary detective novels, happily, even though the stories may be set in Victorian times, the wives of detectives are vital to the success of their husband's investigations, and are acknowledged by everyone as indispensable.

Science fiction is the other popular form in which feminists have had a profound effect. (I ought perhaps to remark here that most writers of detective fiction and science fiction believe themselves to be writing novels. But, as Ursula Le Guin has explained, since you have to be part of a genre to sell, she was willing to call herself the writer of science fiction. That form these days, where it is written by women, involves changes in culture, in family structure, and certainly in all questions of gender. Women writers today of science fiction have, therefore, contrived fascinating utopias. Men today rarely create utopias: as some of us might suggest, they have a utopia right here on earth and must give all their attention to fighting for its preservation.)

Change, you will have gathered, is the dominant mode of these popular forms, and the detectives and explorers of other worlds are all of them fully aware of the changing conditions in their lives and of the unsteadiness of their world. Most women detectives attempt to keep their own balance and concentrate on their visions and imperatives with attention sufficient to maintain them. In detective stories in the old days, that is, before the second half of this century, two modes were evident, the English and the American. In the American a tough male detective, unmarried and with not much use for women, plied his trade on dangerous territory where murder was all too likely to occur. In the English detective novel, which I believe can more properly be called a novel of manners, a highly educated and cultured detective pursued a murderer among a group of persons equally educated and cultured and, in discovering the guilty one, returned the other characters to their accustomed state of innocence,

leaving behind him the upper-class status quo. Both the
American and the English novels, in solving crimes and
punishing the criminal, presented what might be called
the meta-narrative: that is, a puzzle, a solution, a sense of
completion, all-around satisfaction, and the dispersion of
guilt. When the status quo is re-established, no one, least
of all the dective or the suspects, is left in a state of
liminality.

That meta-narrative, like so much else in our current
world, has disappeared. Some men are writing detective
novels with no narrative to speak of; that is to say, the
detective is really the criminal, the criminal is neither
guilty nor to blame, and there is no story trajectory to
follow. For women detective novel writers, the meta-
narrative has been profoundly altered. Although there is a
criminal who is identified at the end, it is clear that he or
she has not indulged in criminality alone, and in identifying the culprit, the woman detective has done something,
if little enough, to change the institution in which the
crime was committed. The new female detective novel no
longer leaves many innocent, and almost always places
the detective in peril. Put otherwise, the woman detective
is undoing the patriarchal structures, bit by bit, and learn-
ing to stay on her feet while the ground shifts beneath her.

The perfect rendition, in my opinion, of how a woman
in science fiction or fantasy works to alter the scheme of
things, is Ursula Le Guin's story 'She Unnames Them.'
Eve, in the garden of Eden, decides to unname the
animals Adam had named, taking this task, with a characteristic male assumption, upon himself. 'Most of the
animals,' Eve reports, 'accepted namelessness with ... perfect indifference.' When none was left to unname, Eve

found the animals 'closer than when their names had
stood between myself and them ... That was more or less
the effect I had been after.' Eve decides to give up her
name too.

> I ... went to Adam, and said 'You and your father lent me
> this – gave it to me, actually. It's been really useful, but it
> doesn't exactly seem to fit very well lately. But thanks very
> much! It's really been very useful' ...
> He was not paying much attention, as it happened, and
> said only, 'Put it down over there, OK?' and went on with
> what he was doing.
> One of the reasons for doing what I did was that talk
> was getting us nowhere, but all the same I felt a little let
> down. I had been prepared to defend my decision. And I
> thought that perhaps when he did notice he might be
> upset and want to talk. I put some things away and fiddled
> around a little, but he continued to do what he was doing
> and to take no notice of anything else. At last I said, 'Well,
> goodbye, dear. I hope the garden key turns up.'
> He was fitting parts together, and said without looking
> around, 'OK, fine, dear. When's dinner?'
> 'I'm not sure,' I said. 'I'm going now. With the —.' I
> hesitated and finally said, 'With them, you know,' and
> went on. In fact, I had only just then realized how hard it
> would have been to explain myself. I could not chatter
> away as I used to do, taking it all for granted. My words
> now must be as slow, as new, as single, as tentative as the
> steps I took going down the path away from the house.[10]

That is as exquisite a distillation of how a marriage changes,
far more brilliant, not to say briefer, than most. But notice

that Eve is uncertain of the future, and has decided against the past. She is, in short, in a state of liminality.

Perhaps some of you know the book *Sophie's World*, subtitled 'A Novel about the History of Philosophy.' In this book, the teacher explains to Sophie, who is fifteen years old, that '[a] philosopher, as we have seen, tries to grasp something that is eternal and immutable.'[11] Feminists, on the other hand, look precisely for what can be changed, ought to be changed, must be changed, for what has wrongly and for too long – even in Plato – been considered immutable. In the higher reaches of academic feminist theory, the state of necessary in-betweenness is understood and valued.

It is my view, and that of many feminist theorists, that there is little point in throwing out the baby with the bath water, that the sensible rethinking and remaking of patriarchal convictions will enable our feminist undertaking. Scepticism is certainly necessary in every case, but why should we not use what we can of the male-designed past, if it will help us. Let us keep those elements which allow us to understand that past and its necessary transformations, but let us not honour them, as Sophie's philosophy teacher does, as 'eternal and immutable.' Postmodernism, in its reconstruction of the past, has supplied us with tools that are applicable to some of the jobs we have to do. In other words, the place of feminism, and women within it, whether philosophers or not, is a place that is amidst, among, atwixt, rooted nowhere except in the realm of questioning, experiment, and adventure, and as it questions everything, it uses what it finds befitting.

Feminists in literature also wish to question established

ideas, but in particular those ideas embodied in traditionally enduring works, that is, in the literary canon. One of the most persistent debates among literary critics is whether great works should be read exclusively as the products of their times, to be analysed only in reference to the ideas prevailing during the lifetime of the author, or whether the very mark of greatness is the capacity of these works to accept and respond to questions asked years, perhaps even centuries, beyond their time. Most feminists, I among them, and many critics not so identified, see this latter capacity as the secret of a work's immortality.

So we academic feminists and literary feminists do not ask for a universal change of the canon. Certainly we believe that works by women and others, long excluded, should now be read as part of the canon. Jane Tompkins's reinstatement of Harriet Beecher Stowe's *Uncle Tom's Cabin* is a good example of this manoeuvre. But beyond the inclusion of previously ignored literature is the necessity of asking new questions of great literature. Many have, for example, noted that Greek literature and English literature are both astonishing in their continued use of women heroes, even though women in both societies had little or no legal power. Why is this? There have been many suggestions, my own being that only women, disempowered and confined to a narrow destiny, could forcefully represent the condition of humanity, even male humanity, which often felt itself in just those circumstances. Consider Antigone, Cassandra, Electra, Clytemnestra, Iphigenia, Athene, Penelope, Hecuba. In English literature, with the exception of the works of Smollett and

Dickens, women have been central from the very beginning, with Moll Flanders, Pamela, and Clarissa. Conrad,
Joyce, and T.S. Eliot, all of them highly suspicious of
women and with no voiced women characters, are not, I
hasten to point out to you, English: they are Polish, Irish,
American.

I have mentioned postmodernist. What of post-femi-
nist? Margaret Atwood has the answer to that. Although
it was published a decade ago, it is as true today as ever.
She wrote, 'The goals of the feminist movement have not
been achieved and those who claim we're living in a post-
feminist era are either sadly mistaken or tired of thinking
about the whole subject.'[12] In my view, not many of us
who have endeavoured to find new answers for the problems of gender are sadly mistaken, but many of us are
tired – and by us I mean not only real people, but characters in literature. Antigone convinced Creon too late; D.H.
Lawrence's Ursula could not satisfy Birkin in marriage,
nor he her; all those heroines who end up in marriage,
with nothing more ever to be heard from them, all those
who in contemporary novels go on alone, not marvellously
happy in their own eyes or in the eyes of society, but more
alive than they would otherwise have been – these may
indeed be tired, if not of 'thinking about the whole subject,' of fighting, and winning, and then having to fight
again.

In the academy we will have to continue to address the
evolving connection between older and younger women
feminists. It is here that a different model than that of
mothers and daughters must emerge. We older feminists
have discovered that we must seek a relationship that is

not modelled on, may not even reflect, the maternal. We have learned that the woman professor cannot hold her own as a maternal figure. On the other hand, the male professor gains from the paternal history of the father who has so long been accepted and internalized as an authority figure by men and women. Women cannot compete as professors within this nuclear family model.

Commerce between younger and older feminists must continue as we search for new ways of relating one to the other. And of course we must not give up. Feminism must continue to be taught, so that today's women students – unlike my generation – when they discover that not all has been won, will have heard it before. They will know that there are books waiting for them as there were no books for me; will know that others have been there, have recorded their experience; will know that help is available and that they can name their anger and find companionship in enduring it. And as for us older feminists in the academy teaching feminism, despite discouragements each day becomes an act of faith.

Let us go back for a moment to my first lecture, to the plain women who, finding no satisfactory place for themselves in the world they were offered, learned to call upon other talents and other attributes, choosing the threshold over societal confirmation. The lessons learned by George Eliot and other nineteenth-century women foretold the experience of all women discontented with the conventional woman's lot and willing to maintain the precarious balance required of those who challenge the given boundaries of a woman's life.

The threshold was never designed for permanent occupation, however, and those of us who occupy thresholds, hover in doorways, and knock upon doors, know that we are in between destinies. But this is where we choose to be, and must be, at this time, among the alternatives that present themselves. And homely or beautiful, real or surrogate mothers, married or unmarried, writers of previously unimagined detectives and travellers in space, we are today, as Adrienne Rich expressed it, finding our way to read and to rewrite 'the book of myths / in which / our names do not appear.'[13]

There can be no doubt that the stationary, conventional place of women, that place ordained by the patriarchy, by male-founded religions, and protected by women who fear anxiety, uncertainty, and liminality, that place occupied by our mothers, will always be attractive to those who would rather be safe than sorry. Yet a life without danger, with no question about what the future may hold, is not a life, it is a carefully structured drama, a play in which our parts are written for us. The threshold, on the contrary, is the place where as women and as creators of literature, we write our own lines and, eventually, our own plays.

NOTES

1 Ann Snitlow, 'A Gender Diary,' in *Conflicts in Feminism*, ed. Marianne Hirsch and Evelyn Fox Keller (New York: Routledge, 1990), 34.
2 Adrienne Rich, *Of Woman Born* (New York: Norton, 1976), 237.
3 Philip Roth, *Patrimony* (New York: Simon & Schuster, 1991), 181.
4 Simone de Beauvoir, *A Very Easy Death*. Translated by Patrick

O'Brien (London: Andre Deutsch, 1965), 89.

5 Dalma Heyn, *Marriage Shock: The Emotional Transformation of Women into Wives* (New York, Villard, 1997), 12.

6 Virginia Woolf, *To the Lighthouse* (New York: Harcourt Brace Jovanovich, 1927), 137.

7 George Bernard Shaw, *The Irrational Knot* (London: Constable, 1909), 220.

8 Quoted in Robert Graves, *Good-bye to All That* (Garden City, NY: Doubleday Anchor, 1957), 272.

9 These last paragraphs on literary marriage are from an essay, 'Marriage Perceived: English Literature 1873–1941,' originally written by me for an early feminist collection, *What Manner of Woman*, ed. Marlene Springer (New York: New York University Press, 1977), 160–83. Rex Stout also identified Watson as a woman and Holmes's wife in 'Watson Was a Woman,' rpt. in Howard Haycroft, *The Art of the Mystery Story* (New York: Grosset & Dunlap, 1947), 311–18.

10 Ursula K. Le Guin, *Buffalo Gals and Other Animal Presences* (New York: New American Library, 1987), 194–6.

11 Jostein Gaarder, *Sophie's World*. Translated by Paulette Moller (New York: Farrar Straus, 1994; rpt. Berkeley Books, 1996), 86.

12 Margaret Atwood, *Second Words* (Boston: Beacon, 1984), 370.

13 In 'Diving into the Wreck.'

THE ALEXANDER LECTURES

The Alexander lectureship was founded in honour of Professor W.J. Alexander, who held the Chair of English at University College, University of Toronto, from 1889 to 1926. The Lectureship brings to the university a distinguished scholar or critic to give a course of lectures on a subject related to English Literature.

1928–9
L.F. Cazamian (Sorbonne): 'Parallelism in the Recent Development of English and French Literature.' Included in *Criticism in the Making* (Macmillan 1929).

1929–30
H.W. Garrod (Oxford): 'The Study of Poetry.' Published as *The Study of Poetry* (Clarendon 1936).

1930–1
Irving Babbit (Harvard): 'Wordsworth and Modern Poetry.' Included in 'The Primitivism of Wordsworth' in *On Being Creative* (Houghton 1932).

1931–2
W.A. Craigie (Chicago): 'The Northern Element in English Literature.' Published as *The Northern Element in English Literature* (University of Toronto Press 1933).

1932–3
H.J.C. Grierson (Edinburgh): 'Sir Walter Scott.' Included in *Sir Walter Scott, Bart* (Constable 1938).

1933–4
G.G. Sedgewick (British Columbia): 'Of Irony, Especially in Drama.'

Published as *Of Irony, Especially in Drama* (University of Toronto Press 1934).

1934–5

E.F. Stoll (Minnesota): 'Shakespeare's Young Lovers.' Published as *Shakespeare's Young Lovers* (Oxford 1937).

1935–6

Franklin B. Snyder (Northwestern): 'Robert Burns.' Included in *Robert Burns, His Personality, His Reputation, and His Art* (University of Toronto Press 1936).

1936–7

D. Nichol Smith (Oxford): 'Some Observations on Eighteenth-Century Poetry.' Published as *Some Observations on Eighteenth-Century Poetry* (University of Toronto Press 1937).

1937–8

Carleton W. Stanley (Dalhousie): 'Matthew Arnold.' Published as *Matthew Arnold* (University of Toronto Press 1938).

1938–9

Douglas Bush (Harvard): 'The Renaissance and English Humanism.' Published as *The Renaissance and English Humanism* (University of Toronto Press 1939).

1939–41

C. Cestre (Paris): 'The Visage of France.' Lectures postponed because of the war and then cancelled.

1941–2

H.J. Davis (Smith): 'Swift and Stella.' Published as *Stella, A Gentlewoman of the Eighteenth Century* (Macmillan 1942).

1942–3

H. Granville-Barker (New York City): 'Coriolanus.' Included in *Prefaces to Shakespeare* volume II (Princeton 1947).

1943–4

F.P. Wilson (Smith): 'Elizabethan and Jacobean.' Published as *Elizabethan and Jacobean* (Clarendon 1945).

1944–5
F.O. Matthiessen (Harvard): 'Henry James: the Final Phase.' Published as *Henry James, the Major Phase* (Oxford 1944).

1945–6
Samuel C. Chew (Bryn Mawr): 'The Virtues Reconciled: A Comparison of Visual and Verbal Imagery.' Published as *The Virtues Reconciled, an Iconographical Study* (University of Toronto Press 1947).

1946–7
Marjorie Hope Nicolson (Columbia): 'Voyages to the Moon.' Published as *Voyages to the Moon* (Macmillan 1948).

1947–8
G.B. Harrison (Queen's): 'Shakespearean Tragedy.' Included in *Shakespeare's Tragedies* (Routledge and Kegan Paul 1951).

1948–9
E.M.W. Tillyard (Cambridge): 'Shakespeare's Problem Plays.' Published as *Shakespeare's Problem Plays* (University of Toronto Press 1949).

1949–50
E.K. Brown (Chicago): 'Rhythm in the Novel.' Published as *Rhythm in the Novel* (University of Toronto Press 1950).

1950–1
Malcolm W. Wallace (Toronto): 'English Character and the English Literary Tradition.' Published as *English Character and the English Literary Tradition* (University of Toronto Press 1952).

1951–2
R.S. Crane (Chicago): 'The Languages of Criticism and the Structure of Poetry.' Published as *The Languages of Criticism and the Structure of Poetry* (University of Toronto Press 1953).

1952–3
V.S. Pritchett. Lectures not given.

1953–4
F.M. Salter (Alberta): 'Mediaeval Drama in Chester.' Published as *Mediaeval Drama in Chester* (University of Toronto Press 1955).

1954–5

Alfred Harbage (Harvard): 'Theatre for Shakespeare.' Published as *Theatre for Shakespeare* (University of Toronto Press 1955).

1955–6

Leon Edel (New York): 'Literary Biography.' Published as *Literary Biography* (University of Toronto Press 1957).

1956–7

James Sutherland (London): 'On English Prose.' Published as *On English Prose* (University of Toronto Press 1957).

1957–8

Harry Levin (Harvard): 'The Question of Hamlet.' Published as *The Question of Hamlet* (Oxford 1959).

1958–9

Bertrand H. Bronson (California): 'In Search of Chaucer.' Published as *In Search of Chaucer* (University of Toronto Press 1960).

1959–60

Geoffrey Bullough (London): 'Mirror of Minds: Changing Psychological Assumptions as Reflected in English Poetry.' Published as *Mirror of Minds: Changing Psychological Beliefs in English Poetry* (University of Toronto Press 1962).

1960–1

Cecil Bald (Chicago): 'The Poetry of John Donne.' Included in *John Donne: A Life* (Oxford 1970).

1961–2

Helen Gardner (Oxford): 'Paradise Lost.' Published as *A Reading of Paradise Lost* (Oxford 1965).

1962–3

Maynard Mack (Yale): 'The Garden and The City: The Theme of Retirement in Pope.' Published as *The Garden and the City* (University of Toronto Press 1969).

1963–4

M.H. Abrams (Cornell): 'Natural Supernaturalism: Idea and Design in Romantic Poetry.' Published as *Natural Supernaturalism* (W.H. Norton 1971).

1964–5
Herschel Baker (Harvard): 'The Race of Time: Three Lectures on Renaissance Historiography.' Published as *The Race of Time* (University of Toronto Press 1967).

1965–6
Northrop Frye (Toronto): 'Fools of Time: Studies in Shakespearian Tragedy.' Published as *Fools of Time* (University of Toronto Press 1967).

1967–8
Frank Kermode (Bristol): 'Criticism and English Studies.'

1967–8
Francis E. Mineka (Cornell): 'The Uses of Literature, 1750–1850.'

1968–9
H.D.F. Kitto (Bristol): 'What is Distinctively Hellenic in Greek Literature?'

1968–9
W.J. Bate (Harvard): '*The Burden of the Past and the English Poet* (1660–1840).' Published as *The Burden of the Past and the English Poet* (Belknap 1970).

1970–1
J.A.W. Bennett (Cambridge): 'Chaucer at Oxford and at Cambridge.' Published as *Chaucer at Oxford and at Cambridge* (University of Toronto Press 1974).

1971–2
Roy Daniels (British Columbia): 'Mannerism: An Inclusive Art Form.'

1972–3
Hugh Kenner (California): 'The Meaning of Rhyme.' Publication planned.

1973–4
Ian Watt (Stanford): 'Four Western Myths.' Publication planned.

1974–5
Richard Ellmann (Oxford): 'The Consciousness of Joyce.' Published as *The Consciousness of Joyce* (Oxford 1977).

1975–6

Henry Nash Smith (Berkeley): 'Other Dimensions: Hawthorne, Melville, and Twain.' Included in *Democracy and the Novel: Popular Resistance to Classic American Writers* (Oxford 1978).

1976–7

Kathleen Coburn (Toronto): 'Some Perspectives on Coleridge.' Published as *Experience into Thought: Perspectives in the Coleridge Notebooks* (University of Toronto Press 1979).

1977–8

E.P. Thompson (Worcester): 'William Blake: Tradition and Revolution 1789–1793.' Publication planned.

1978–9

Ronald Paulson (Yale): 'The Representation of Revolution 1789–1820.' Published as *The Representation of Revolution* (1789–1820) (Yale 1983).

1979–80

David Daiches (Edinburgh): 'Literature and Gentility in Scotland.' Published as *Literature and Gentility in Scotland.* (Edinburgh 1982).

1980–1

Walter J. Ong., sj (St. Louis): 'Hopkins, the Self, and God.' Published as *Hopkins, the Self, and God* (University of Toronto Press 1986).

1982

Robertson Davies (Toronto): 'The Mirror of Nature.' Published as *The Mirror of Nature* (University of Toronto Press 1983).

1983

Anne Barton (Cambridge): 'Comedy and the Naming of Parts.' Published as *The Names of Comedy* (University of Toronto Press 1990).

1984

Guy Davenport (Kentucky): 'Objects on a Table: Still Life in Literature and Painting.'

1985

Richard Altick (Ohio): 'The Victorian Sense of the Present.'

1986

Jerome J. McGann (California): Various Subjects

1987

Inga-Stina Ewbank (London): 'The World and the Theatre: Strindberg, Ibsen and Shakespeare.'

1988

Christopher Ricks (Boston): 'Allusion and Inheritance 1784–1824.'

1989

John Burrow (Bristol): 'Langland's *Piers Plowman*: The Uses of Fiction.' Published as *Langland's Fictions* (Oxford 1993).

1990

John Fraser (Dalhousie): 'Nihilism, Modernism, and Value.'

1991

Mary Jacobus (Cornell): 'First Things: Reproductive Origins.'

1992

Peter Conrad (Oxford): 'To Be Continued ...'

1993

V.A. Kolve (California): 'The God-Denying Fool in Medieval Art and Drama.'

1994

Samuel Hynes (Princeton): 'The Soldiers' Tale: Narratives of War in the Twentieth Century.' Published as *The Soldiers' Tale: Bearing Witness to Modern War* (Lane 1997).

1995

Gillian Beer (Cambridge): 'Scaling the Island.'

1996

Paul Fussell (Pennsylvania): 'In Search of Modernism.'

1997

Carolyn G. Heilbrun (Columbia): 'Women's Lives: The View from the Threshold.' Published as *Women's Lives: The View from the Threshold* (University of Toronto Press 1999).